W9-CPC-955

*Death Before Dishonor*

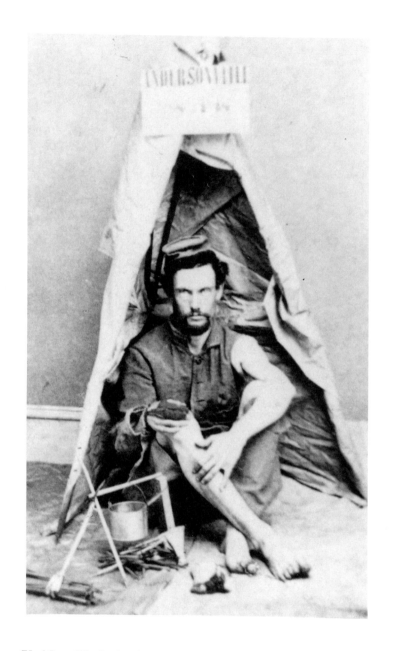

Unidentified Andersonville survivor, taken by a
Paterson, N.J. photographer.

# DEATH BEFORE DISHONOR

## The Andersonville Diary of Eugene Forbes
## 4th New Jersey Infantry

Edited by William B. Styple

Belle Grove Publishing Co.

# Table of Contents

# Acknowledgments

130 years ago, the diary written by Eugene Forbes was printed as a 68-page pamphlet and few copies are in existence today. For this expanded work, I would like to thank the following people who shared letters, diaries and photographs of soldiers from the 4th New Jersey Infantry. Thank you all for your help.

Marie Louise Stokes provided a treasure of information on Robert S. Johnston and Company B. Dennis Buttacavoli shared his collection of letters that were written by Robert Aiken. Joe Bilby was of great help by providing accounts of the 4th New Jersey and also by contributing the Forbes letter detailing the Battle of Crampton's Gap. John Kuhl generously allowed me to publish photographs from his personal collection. Charles Webster of the Trenton Public Library was of great assistance with research on John P. Beech. Thanks go to Rob Hodge who assisted in researching the pension and service records at the National Archives--he made my job a lot easier. I would like to thank also the staffs at the New Jersey Historical Society and the New Jersey State Archives for all their service.

Special thanks go to Andrea Wilkerson, Ed Colimore, Sonia Krutzke, Buddy Kruk, Bob Crickenberger, Jack Fitzpatrick, Bill Dekker, Bruce Jones, Larry Sangi, Jim Nevins, Bill Mapes, and Brian Pohanka for help in preparing this book. Most of all, I would like to thank my wife Nancy for her endless help and support.

My father, a veteran of World War II, passed away while I was editing this book and if it is appropriate, I would like to dedicate this volume to the memory of Edward Styple.

# Introduction

In the trenches around Petersburg, Va., on March 22, 1865, Sergeant John P. Beech, Co. B 4th N.J., Infantry wrote in his diary:

"Saw in a Trenton paper the death of Sergeant Eugene Forbes, at Florence, South Carolina, where he died of systematic starvation. He was the soul of honor and a more patriotic man never lived. He was an orphan and enlisted at the outbreak of the war in the three-months men then in our Company B for three years. He was captured on the 6th of May, 1864, in the Wilderness, when the rebels got around our right flank. He was of frail build and many a time on our long marches some of the boys would help him to keep up by carrying his gun or knapsack. He could have had a commission but refused it. He was a printer and kept a diary, seeing which prompted me to do so."

Remarkably, the diary that Eugene Forbes kept survived the ordeal though he did not. After Forbes was buried as an unknown in a mass grave, a fellow prisoner brought the carefully preserved diary back to Trenton. He gave it to Messrs. Phillips & Boswell, Forbes's former employers, who had it printed as a pamphlet in 1865. The diary is the voice of Sergeant Eugene Forbes from the grave, and serves as a testimony to the horrors of prison life during the Civil War. While many former prisoners wrote of their wartime experiences, several accounts have been criticized as inaccurate, embroidered, or written for profit. This is not true of the Forbes diary. No one can accuse Forbes of waving the bloody shirt, or trying to profit from his wartime experiences.

Eugene Forbes was born on May 14, 1833, in Trenton, N.J. His enlistment papers indicate that he was five feet seven inches in height with blue eyes, light hair, and a light complexion. Unfortunately, no photographic portrait of him is known to exist. Though John Beech believed Forbes to be an orphan, there is one small passage in Forbes' diary that suggests otherwise. On June 5, 1864, Forbes mentions briefly that he "wrote a short note to mother." It is the only mention he makes of any family back home.

Aside from his 1864 diary, Forbes left behind very little written material about his service. Two letters written by him have been recently discovered and are reproduced in these pages. But to fully understand the Forbes diary and his four years of soldiering, excerpts of letters and diaries from comrades, in Company B 4th N.J. Infantry, are utilized throughout the introduction to better tell the story.

On April 15, 1861, after the firing on Fort Sumter in Charleston harbor, President Abraham Lincoln issued his first call for troops. New Jersey's quota was four regiments of three-month militia. Governor Charles S. Olden issued his proclamation to the State and the citizens volunteered with enthusiasm.

Eugene Forbes was among the first of these volunteers, enlisting in Company D, 3rd New Jersey Militia. The brigade of Jerseymen rushed to Washington to defend against a threatened Rebel invasion. One of the volunteers recorded in his journal,

"This afternoon (May 7), at short notice, the whole New Jersey Brigade was paraded and marched to the White House, where we were reviewed by the President, General [Winfield] Scott, and members of the Cabinet. It is seldom that four regiments of soldiers have appeared on parade together in this country, and it was a novel sight to the citizens of Washington."

In order to safeguard Washington, it was necessary to occupy the Virginia side of the Potomac River. Just past midnight on May 24th, the 3rd, 2nd and 4th New Jersey regiments started for Virginia. "The moon was shining brightly", wrote one member of the 3rd, "The long lines filed slowly out of camp and down the road, their bayonets gleaming in the moonlight, and no sound save the measured tramp of nearly a thousand feet. At ten minutes before three o'clock our feet struck the soil of old Virginia."

After the Union defeat at Bull Run on July 21, 1861, the 90 day enlistments expired for the New Jersey Militia. As the soldiers returned home, many volunteered in the three year regiments then being raised. Upon his arrival in Trenton, Forbes wasted no time and enlisted in Company B, 4th New Jersey Volunteer Infantry. The 85 men of Company B included two neighborhood fire companies and a group of workers from a Trenton pottery. William Seddon, a potter who boasted of Crimean War service with the British Army, was elected captain. A friend of Forbes, Robert S. Johnston of the Eagle Fire Company, was elected First Lieutenant, and on August 9th, Forbes was mustered in as a private.

The 4th New Jersey Infantry, 909 strong, traveled to Washington and Alexandria where the regiment joined the 1st, 2nd, and 3rd Volunteer Regiments, under the command of Brigadier General Philip Kearny. The First New Jersey Brigade was encamped at St. John's Episcopal Seminary, some three miles from Alexandria. For the next seven months Eugene Forbes, and his comrades of Company B, learned to be soldiers and occasionally skirmished with the enemy. During this time, Forbes was promoted to the rank of Corporal. On one occasion Captain Seddon and his potters, dressed in fatigue coats and camp hats, posed casually for a visiting photographer in front of their Sibley tents. Later, a more formal photograph of the entire company was taken at Dress Parade. Somewhere amongst the men of Company B, Corporal Eugene Forbes stands at rest.

In March 1862, the First New Jersey Brigade of General William Franklin's Division, Army of the Potomac, readied for the coming spring campaign. After an advance and brief occupation of the abandoned Confederate defenses at Manassas, the brigade accompanied army commander General George B. McClellan's expedition to the Virginia peninsula to capture the Confederate capitol. As the men readied to embark on the transports, Company B lost its commander. Captain Seddon deserted taking Corporal Elijah Heath with him. It was reported that the two men fled to New York, then to England or Australia. Private Robert Aitken, of Company B, angrily called it, "a damn

Here is a group of Trenton potters who served in the defense of the Union in 1861. They were members of Company B., Fourth Regiment, New Jersey Volunteers, and of the group only three are living today. This photograph was taken at Camp Seminary, Va., 1861. Those seen in the picture are, reading from left to right: Sergeant Jacob Osterman, Sergeant Robert Ellis, John Wood, John Barlow, Thomas Leonard, Corporal Joseph Lawton, Ames Voorhees, Sergeant Thomas McNulty, Captain William Seddon, Ralph Owen, Hugh McLaughlin, Joseph Beech, Henry Lawton, John Nelson, Samuel Farrell, John P. Beech, John Pittisen, Isaac Fielding, Corporal Elijah Heath, Arthur McReavy and Sergeant John Machin. In the background are seen Second Lieutenant Fred Arrisen of Company F., and a number of other onlookers who were not potters. All of the above-named are deceased with the exception of Joseph Lawton, Henry Lawton and John Beech, mouldmakers. Joseph Lawton, of 59 Garfield avenue, will receive $2 for the loan of this photograph.

## (Top) Taken from the State Gazette, June 10, 1922.
## (Bottom) Co. B at Dress Parade

mean trick." First Lieutenant Johnston assumed command of the Company. "I am tolerably liked by the men," he wrote to his wife, "and they put a good deal of confidence in me."

As the First New Jersey Brigade toiled through the swamps of the peninsula, illness took its inevitable toll in the ranks. In a letter home, Private Aitken wrote, "Lieut. Bob Johnston has been sick for some time in the hospital. We have but one officer to take command of us. [Lt. Josiah Shaw] If we should be called into action, we would fare bad for I think he is very thick headed."

From his sickbed, Lieutenant Johnston wrote his wife:

"There was another man died yesterday from fever. This makes four in a few days from this Regt. They average one death daily. We have quite a grave yard here and a great many sick. All these deaths since we came here two weeks ago, are horrible, horrible. Poor men dying away from home from those that is dear to them. God forbid that I should be a victim of death in this place."

Aside from a few light skirmishes, the 4th regiment's baptism of fire would prove to be unlucky. Frank W. Gaul of the 4th wrote some years after the war,

"Our first engagement of any importance was at Gaines's Mills, 27th of June 1862, in McClellan's Campaign on the Peninsula, where our regiment with the 11th Pennsylvania Reserves were sent in as a forlorn hope to cover the retreat of the army, and where both regiments were captured, entirely, after using sixty rounds of ammunition, all they had."

John Beech, Forbes' fellow diarist in Company B, gave a more detailed account of the battle of Gaines's Mill:

"We advanced with a yell a short distance, halted and opened and maintained a most murderous fire. We were armed with the new Springfield rifle with patent cartridge (no biting of cartridges). Our fire was rapid and incessant. Line after line of the enemy was broken, as admitted by them later.

"About seven o'clock, after several requests from Colonel [Thomas F.] Gallagher, of the 11th Pennsylvania, he was allowed to relieve us, our ammunition being about expended. We marched out of the woods, faced to the rear into the clearing about fifty yards, the ground having a gentle decline from the edge of the woods. To the left, on higher ground, was an old bush-camp, about a hundred or a hundred and fifty yards distant. A long line of battle was drawn up facing us. Out of the woods to their left a column of troops, at double-quick, was going into the line on their right. The smoke of burnt powder was so dense that it was hard to tell whether they were our supports or the enemy. Lieutenant Josiah Shaw, of Company B, undertook to find out and proceeded towards the line of battle, running. He had advanced about half way when he was fired upon, the bullet cutting his sword belt. This was sufficient to show that they were the enemy and in our rear. Colonel [James H.] Simpson attempted to take the regiment past the enemy's right flank, through the bush camp, but the enemy at once prepared to deliver a volley. The order to lie down was promptly obeyed, and the volley passed harmlessly over them, but caught the 11th Pennsylvania in the rear. This was the first the Pennsylvania regiment knew of the enemy being in their rear, and almost at the same moment their foes charged them in front. This regiment was forced back from their line, into and over the 4th New Jersey. It being certain that escape was impossible, the 4th Regiment surrendered to the 4th Texas, of General Whiting's division. We had been fighting for over an hour after all the other regiments of the Union army had been withdrawn, at least ten times our number, and had kept the enemy from advancing to the capture of the bridge. We went into the fight with less than 600 men, and our losses were 52 killed outright or mortally wounded, 103 wounded and 437 captured."

After the disaster at Gaines's Mill, the men of the 4th along with the 11th Pennsylvania were marched into Richmond. Charles F. Currie, of the 4th, later wrote,

"[We] were escorted to Richmond, being the first two regiments of the Union army to enter Richmond, not voluntarily however. In going through the streets of Richmond with our escorts we were subjected to all sorts of indignities, the worst of which was trailing our colors through the streets in front of us." Robert Aitken of Company B wrote, "it was a bitter pill to swallow, to stand to see the Damned Rebels take our colors. It made my blood boil, but we could do nothing."

The soldiers found themselves first at Libby Prison, where after some weeks the enlisted men were transferred to Belle Isle in the James River. This would be the first taste of prison life for Eugene Forbes, and for the next 42 days he endured the hardships of captivity. One of Forbes' comrades later reminisced about confinement on Belle Isle:

"Sometimes men who were crazed by fever and suffering would attempt to escape. Robert Love, of Company G, was one of these. He made a desperate rush and succeeded in passing both lines of guards, and threw himself into the James, striking out for the opposite shore. Of course the alarm was given at once, and in a few minutes the shore was lined with guards, each shooting at the bold man who was swimming across the stream. There must have been at least a hundred guards, each firing as fast as he could load, but strange to say, not a shot reached the mark. By the time poor Love, thoroughly exhausted, reached the opposite shore, there were plenty of 'rebs' there to meet him. The poor fellow was brought back, put in irons, and died shortly afterward."

Following the clash at Gaines's Mill, General George McClellan continued his controversial "change of base" across the peninsula. His army had to abandon great amounts of supplies and all types of small arms. These weapons, coveted by the Confederacy, were brought to Richmond, where someone conceived the idea of having them cleaned by the Union prisoners on Belle Isle. Each prisoner was promised an extra ration of bread for this labor. Charles F. Currie, later wrote, "This was a great temptation, under the circumstances, but so far as I know only one yielded to the seductive offer, and he only worked one day. As soon as he came into camp that night one side of his head was shaved and he was given a sound thrashing by his disgusted comrades."

After seven weeks imprisonment, Forbes and his comrades were exchanged at Aiken's Landing. The 4th Regiment's numbers were greatly reduced. Upon arriving at Alexandria, less than 500 men were present for duty, many too weak for the rigors of campaigning. As the regiment was being reorganized, the soldiers were supplied with inadequate smoothbore muskets. The soldiers grumbled about the loss of their fine Springfield rifled muskets and regimental flags at Gaines's Mill. Above all, they wanted an opportunity to avenge their disgrace in battle.

On August 27th, with Stonewall Jackson's troops raiding the Union supply depot at Manassas Junction, the First New Jersey Brigade was sent by rail to reconnoiter. John Beech recorded in his diary:

"As we got off the cars we heard heavy firing in the direction of Bull Run. The Brigade marched up to Bull Run bridge. General [George W.] Taylor took the 1st, 2nd and 3rd Regiments and advanced towards the heights beyond, leaving the 4th Regiment to hold the bridge. Nine companies held the bridge, while the other (my company B,) was deployed along Bull Run as Skirmishers to the right of the bridge, to prevent a flank attack."

After a sharp fight, the First New Jersey Brigade was soundly defeated by Jackson's troops. The much desired retribution for the humiliation of Gaines's Mill would come two weeks later, in Maryland, at Crampton's Gap in South Mountain.

The following letter, describing the battles of Crampton's Gap and Antietam, Md., was written by Eugene Forbes and sent to an unidentified friend in Trenton.

**Post-war photograph of John Beech, Co. B 4th NJV.**

Crampton Gap, Blue Ridge Mts.,
Near Middleton, Md., Sept. 16, 1862

I am going to begin this letter but the Lord only knows when I will get it done. So if I seem to break it off short, you may believe that we have marched in a hurry, or something of the kind.

Well we licked 'em. We did but we had to fight for it. Our loss is not heavy, but it is only by God's good Providence that there are one hundred men left in the Brigade. Our Regiment fought nobly. Our Sergeant [Jacob Osterman], was wounded in the thigh, and Samuel S. Hull, the best man, and the only true Christian in the company, was killed by a rifle ball through the throat. He died while praying.

We started Sunday morning, about ten o'clock, and marched some eight miles, crossing a range of mountains which I suppose is a spur of the Blue Ridge. When we reached the top of the mountain, the road lead along its side for a quarter of a mile, and we had a splendid view of the country around and below us, Crampton Gap, where we now are, and where we shortly afterwards won a most brilliant victory. It is a magnificent country. For miles below us, was spread a level plain, dotted here and there with farm houses, and two or three thriving little villages. We advanced over the level country, and halted within a mile or so of the foot of the mountain on which the rebels were posted. Most of the division[1st Division, Sixth Corps] was stationed in a deep hollow, out of sight of the rebels, but our brigade was up on the side of the hills, and the rebels threw a couple of shells so near us that we moved down with the rest of the division. Our artillery threw half a dozen shells into the woods, and when the rebel position had been ascertained we were moved out of the hollow, and formed line-of-battle in an open field, in view of the rebels, and advanced in line-of-battle, crossing two open fields and a corn field, and then another open field, and then we opened fire on them from behind a stone wall, with a fence on top of it. They were hid in the bushes, and behind stone walls and fences. Soon we got the order to charge bayonets, and double quick, and away we went over the fences and across the fields yelling like a pack of devils. The rebel shells came pouring thick and fast. But it was no use. They could not stand it but started up the mountain, and and we gained the stone wall they had fired from. We fired a few rounds until we got our breath again, and then away we went again, charging over the fence again and driving them up the mountain. By this time the regiments were all broken up, and every man fighting on his own hook. We drove them up one mountain on one side of the gap, then down into the gap, and up the mountain on the other side, and down that, took two cannon, about one thousand prisoners, and a large number of small arms. I have heard no estimate of our loss yet, but the rebels lay dead thickly over the mountains, and behind the fences where they had fought. Our Adjutant was killed. Our regiment would not make two full companys now, and the second regiment also suffered severely. We have been laying still since, but the fighting has been going around us, and we expect to be called on any moment. It was more terrible to me to go over the mountain and hear the poor wounded rebels crying for water which was almost impossible to get, and asking us to pray for them, than it was for me to face the heaviest fire we were under that day. I gave one poor fellow a drink from my canteen, and he threw his arms around my neck and prayed God to bless me. He was mortally wounded and probably died in half an hour. Another to whom I gave water was a young boy, apparently fifteen years old, and a beautiful youth, though very pale from loss of blood. He was shot through the thigh. The wounded have all been taken care of now, but the dead are not all buried yet, though our men and the sesech prisoners have been busy working night and day. We did not get poor Hull buried till this morning. One of our Captains had to be carried from the field before we got in rifle range, from palpitation of the heart. He has shown the white feather on several occasions. I'll bet he didn't have it worse than I did before I got to the top of the first mountain, but I stuck to it, though I had to lean my back against a tree twice to fire my piece, before I got to the top. If I had given palpitation of the heart, as an excuse, I would have been called a coward, but I suppose it ain't cowardice in a Captain--Oh, Moses!

Monday we layed still and picked up the wounded, buried the dead and sent prisoners in until they amounted to 907. If we had cavalry we would have taken 2,000. On Tuesday we had a heavy rain, and laid down under arms all night wet through. On Wednesday we marched some seven or eight miles, over beautiful country till we came to where there had been severe fighting. Dead men and horses were lying in groups through the woods and fields along the roadside. Houses had been torn to pieces by shells and shot, and all things bare the marks of war. We were placed to support a battery, or rather, two or three of them. We laid down on our faces in a plowed field, all day, the enemy's shells bursting directly over us, and their solid shot plowing the ground around and among us. One of our men had his cap knocked off by a cannon ball, and a piece of shell struck within two inches of another's head, but fortunately no one in our company was hurt, though several were wounded in the brigade. It is a great deal more trying to the courage and nerves of a man to lie behind a battery of artillery all day and have the shells and balls bursting and falling around him, than it is to charge against infantry and artillery together.　In the one case the mind has nothing to occupy it, but the expectation of being struck, in the other case, the excitement of charging overcame the sensation of fear.　But we licked 'em again, and that night they skedaddled for Virginia, at least the greatest part of them.　The next day the truce was granted to bury the dead, and pick up the wounded, and Thursday night they all left, giving us a couple shot on Friday by the way of a parting salute.　They left hundreds of their dead unburied.　In some places they laid piled on top of each other for several feet, so close that you could not step between them. Towards noon we followed up the retreat.　We arrived at Nolan's Ferry on Friday afternoon, and I have written this sheet today, (Saturday).　There was a heavy cannonading further along the river, and some pieces of railroad iron thrown by the rebs, reached our camps, but all is quiet this P.M.　I have not time to write more.　If the mail does not go to-day, I will write more.

Good-bye

Eugene

Captain Robert S. Johnston promoted Corporal Forbes to the rank of Sergeant after the battle of Crampton's Gap.

For the next several weeks the Union army remained inactive in Maryland. On October 4th, during an inspection by General McClellan's chief of staff, General Randolph B. Marcy, Company B drew the officer's attention. Capt. Johnston described the notice to his wife, "My company got the praise of being the best in the Regiment, and passed quite a compliment on me for having such a company."

The inaction of the Army of the Potomac caused General McClellan's removal. John Beech wrote, "It was about time. We do not know anything about the abilities of his successor (Gen. Burnside) but he cannot be a greater failure than McClellan."

Honor was restored to the 4th Regiment on December 9th when a new stand of colors was presented from the State of New Jersey. Colonel William Hatch, who Capt. Johnston said, "put on more airs than a French Prince" made an acceptance speech and the men saluted the flags and cheered. The State flag was inscribed with the legend,

*"Presented by the State of New Jersey*
*To her Fourth Regiment*
*For Gallant Conduct at Crampton's Pass, Maryland,*
*September 14th 1862."*

Two days later, the army was marching to Fredericksburg. One soldier of the 4th New Jersey wrote in his diary, "The roads were at first in splendid condition, but by mid-day became intolerably muddy, onward we moved til within an hour's march of Fredericksburg. The city at this time was already partly in flames."

On December 13th, the 4th Regiment, only 300 strong, was ordered to advance and drive the enemy from a railroad cut south of Fredericksburg. "The troops advanced in a handsome manner under a severe fire," wrote brigade commander General Alfred Torbert, "and then charged the enemy's position, led by their gallant leader, Colonel William Hatch, driving them from it with great loss, capturing about 25 prisoners of a Georgia and North Carolina Regiment." A Confederate brigade then counterattacked and drove the Jerseymen out of the railroad cut with severe losses. The 4th New Jersey suffered 80 casualties at Fredericksburg, including Colonel Hatch, who was mortally wounded.

In January, 1863, Burnside's Army of the Potomac tried once again to maneuver against the Confederates at Fredericksburg. This time they were defeated by the elements. Captain Johnston, in a letter to his wife, described the infamous "mud march":

"The day we marched it commenced raining. The more it rained, the worse the roads became, and the first night we halted in a woods, pitched our small tents on the damp leaves and erecting large fires. While drying one side of ourselves, the other was getting wet. The second day we made slow progress, the roads by this time had become a slush pond. Finally night came and we halted again, still raining. The third day we did not move. Our Artillery was unmovable and so was our supply trains, ammunition trains and pontoons. So here we are stuck in the mud."

What followed was much needed reorganization for the demoralized Union army. General Hooker replaced Burnside and in April, the 4th Regiment was detached from the Jersey Brigade and sent to army headquarters where three companies under Lieutenant Colonel Charles Ewing were assigned to provost guard duty, and Colonel William Birney with seven companies (including Company B) guarded the reserve artillery ammunition train at army headquarters. The men welcomed this easy duty. On June 12th, Colonel Birney resigned, and Captain Johnston, being the senior captain, assumed command of the battalion. On June 14th, Johnston promoted his friend Forbes to Quartermaster Sergeant of the 4th New Jersey.

Meanwhile, Company B continued to guard the wagon train as the Army of the Potomac marched to counter Lee's invasion of the North, which culminated in the battle of Gettysburg. John Beech wrote of their role in the battle:

"We left Taneytown, Md., at 8 am and arrived at Gettysburg a little after noon. Between two and three o'clock, Longstreet made his flank assault. Then our regiment doublequicked and deployed to stop the fugitives coming across the fields, with our right resting on the Baltimore Pike. After the panic subsided, we retired and moved our train further to the rear as the enemy shells were falling among the train." On the third day of the battle, Company B was sent to Westminster, Md., to escort an ammunition train on its way to Gettysburg.

Following the battle, it was necessary for an eight-man recruiting detail from the 4th to return to Trenton and fill its depleted ranks. Capt. Robert Johnston was assigned this coveted duty. While at home, he received a letter from now Private Eugene Forbes with the latest news from the regiment.

Camp in the Field, Va.,
Near Culpepper C.H.
Sept. 18, 1863
Dear Captain:

I received yours of the 14th inst last night. This may not reach you for several days, as our mails are very irregular. I am glad to hear that you continue in good health, and wish I could say as much for myself.

There is no doubt but that some of the officers envy your position, but I have heard none of them express any dissatisfaction. Perhaps if they could oust you, some of them would attempt it, but I do not think any of them will venture to try it.

I have been intending to write you for some days but my ill health and this march, has prevented me. But, "better late then never." The boys generally appear better satisfied in the Brigade than they were in the reserve, though they have had it pretty rough so far.

It seems to be the impression here that you will get the vacant Majority. You certainly should and unless politics have more to do with the matter than merit and patriotism, which is too often the case, you will get it. I wish you success.

As for myself, I have been promoted--Backwards--and am now a "high private in the rear rank." I certainly deserved reduction for many transgressions of which I was guilty, but though nominally I was reduced for drunkeness, actually other causes produced the result. The day we left the reserve to return to the Brigade, Lieut. [Dillwyn] Purington informed me that I was to be reduced to the rank of sergeant and sent to my company the 1st of September. This was on Aug. 24th, the Lieut. said I did not suit the Major as Qr. Mstr. Sgt. and that I would be reduced and

**Robert S. Johnston Co. B 4th N.J.V.**

**Unidentified New Jersey soldiers at the Trenton Barracks, 1863.**

finally made a 1st Sgt. of Co. B. I told him I would not take that position. He gave me a canteen of liquor and I drinked considerable, but not so much. But I was able to get to Warrenton with the train, return to the Junction with a wagon we had borrowed to carry some of the goods, and again get to Warrenton at sundown. So you see I did a pretty fair days work. But as luck would have it, the Major's orderly lost a bottle of rum from his saddle bag, and suspicion fastened upon me, I suppose because it was evident I had been drinking. On the 26th August, Purington left a note with the Adjutant, and on the 26th I was reduced by an order. But let it slide. I can work through my eleven months. I feel much better satisfied in the Company than I did as Qr. Mstr. Srgt., and it is not for a great while anyhow.

This part of Virginia does not look as if any troops had ever been here. Corn and fence rails are very plenty, but the supply is fast diminishing before the inroads of the Northern barbarians.

Well, Captain you must be tired of reading this scrawl. I know I am tired of scribbling sitting tailor fashion. If you see any of my people, tell them I am all right, and ask John Gildea when he is going to pay me that dollar I owe him.

Good Bye now, and write a few lines occasionally to

Yours Respy.<br>Eugene

Forbes's reduction in ranks did not last long, for he was promoted Corporal on October 1, 1863. In late November, the First New Jersey Brigade was encamped at Brandy Station, Va., and took part in the bitter cold Mine Run Campaign. Towards Christmas, most of the 4th New Jersey Infantry, whose term of enlistment would expire the following August, chose to reenlist for three years or the duration of the war. As an incentive for reenlisting, the men were given a thirty-day veteran furlough. Having regained his sergeant's stripes, Forbes began his furlough on New Year's Day, 1864.

One veteran of the 4th later wrote, "Went home for thirty days; had the time of our lives; returned when our time was up, and rejoined the Brigade where we left them, at Brandy Station, and continued in the business of making history."

The history that was to be made was to be the bloodiest campaign of the Civil War, and for Sergeant Eugene Forbes, a struggle for survival in the most infamous of all wartime prison camps--Andersonville.

Andersonville, Elmira, Libby, Fort Delaware, Belle Isle, Point Lookout, are names of prison camps that will forever be identified with suffering, cruelty and death. Of the 620,000 deaths during the Civil War, over 60,000 soldiers perished in prison camps.

In the first two years of the conflict each side agreed upon terms for parole and an exchange of captured prisoners of war. A "parole" was a prisoner's pledge of honor not to take up arms, nor to participate in the war in any way. In the beginning, captives were seldom interned, but were held for a time or simply sent home until exchanges could be negotiated. Once a prisoner was exchanged, he was released from parole and could return to his regiment.

By the fall of 1863, this system broke down due to misunderstandings and abuses. Exchanges were suspended and both sides prepared for an influx of prisoners in the upcoming campaigns of 1864 as U. S. Grant met Robert E. Lee in the Virginia Wilderness, and William T. Sherman advanced through Georgia against Joseph Johnston. Though negotiations were held throughout 1864, both governments failed to reach an agreement on the exchange of prisoners. Each fixed blame on the other and as a result, thousands of soldiers died.

Fearing cavalry raids on Richmond, Confederate officials chose a site deep in southwest Georgia near the railroad depot of Andersonville to construct a new prison. Camp Sumter, or more commonly known as Andersonville, received its first 500 prisoners on February 25, 1864, even before the stockade had been finished.

The walls of the stockade were constructed of pine logs 22 feet in length, set five feet in the ground and stood 17 feet above it. Initially, the enclosed area was about 16.5 acres. There were two entrances into the stockade, both on the west side, which were called the North and South Gates. For observation, sentry boxes or "pigeon-roosts" were erected on the outer side of the stockade at intervals of 40 yards. Inside the pen a "deadline" was established 19 feet from the wall. It was marked by a three-foot-tall railing which no prisoner was allowed to cross under the penalty of being shot.

Upon arrival at Andersonville, prisoners were organized into 270 man detachments, divided into three 90-man squads, each subdivided into three 30-man messes. A sergeant was placed in charge of each detachment. After entering the stockade, it was a prisoner's responsibility to provide his own shelter. Many had only what was carried on their backs. Space had to be found and rude shelters or "shebangs" were erected by the prisoners. Countless times, a new arrival or "fresh fish" would be pounced upon, robbed and sometimes killed by gangs of fellow prisoners known as Raiders. When these thieves grew more powerful and brazen, they were challenged by the law-and-order group of prisoners called Regulators. With the help of Confederate authorities the raiders were arrested, tried by a court of prisoners, convicted, and six of the leaders hanged.

The main water supply for the prison was a stream called the Stockade Branch of Sweetwater Creek which flowed from west to east. It passed first through the camps of Confederate guards, who used it as a latrine, then by the cookhouse where grease and refuse were dumped in, and finally it entered the stockade where it supplied drinking and washing water for the prisoners. Sinks were built for the camp latrine near the east wall, but the sluggish stream was not swift enough to carry away the voidings of 25,000 prisoners and a large swamp of liquid filth resulted. Besides giving off a horrible stench, the stream soon became a breeding ground for maggots, mosquitoes and infection of all types. Lice were plentiful, and the prisoners spent hours "skirmishing" or picking lice from their clothes.

By June the population exceeded 25,000, far more than the number the prison was designed to hold. The Confederates sought to alleviate the overcrowding by enlarging the stockade to the north by 10 acres. A work crew of 130 prisoners completed the project on June 30, and 13,000 prisoners were designated to relocate to the expanded area. On the morning of July 2nd, the entire old north wall had disappeared, scavenged by the prisoners for building materials and fuel.

In the last week of July there were 29,998 prisoners being held in the stockade. In August, there were 32,899 prisoners, with deaths totaling 2,993 for that month. The largest number of deaths in a single day (127) occurred on August 23rd.

After Sherman captured Atlanta in September, worried Confederate authorities began to transport the Andersonville prisoners to other locations. Many were sent to Florence, South Carolina where an Andersonville-style prison was built. By most accounts the conditions at Florence were worse than Andersonville.

After the war, Warren Lee Goss, wrote of captivity at Florence:

"In November the cold became so intense, our rations so inadequate for the maintenance of health, the prospects of an exchange before the close of the war so vague, and the chances for life so uncertain, that the strongest heart recoiled at the thoughts of the future. Broken in health and spirits, they cast despairingly around them in search of some means by which to escape from the impending doom which threatened them. Terrible were those days and nights of torture and death, from which there seemed no release.  Most of the prisoners whose hearts had been buoyed so long by hope of exchange, parole, or deliverance by raids, now sank in despondency.  Taking advantage of this hopelessness among prisoners, a recruiting station for the Confederate army was opened near the stockade, the officers of which came into prison for recruits.  There were some among us so helpless, so lost to every feeling but hunger, that they bartered their honor for food, and took the oath of allegiance to the detested Confederacy.  Many died rather than stain their lips with the dishonor of such an oath."

By refusing to take the oath of allegiance to the Confederacy, Sergeant Eugene Forbes chose to perish with his honor intact.  "I will lay my bones in this accursed soil," Forbes wrote, "rather than ever assume a semblance of respect or allegiance to this hellborn conspiracy against one of the best, if not the very best, earthly governments that ever existed.  God bless it."  Forbes died on February 7, 1865.  God bless him.

**William B. Styple**
**Kearny, N.J.**
**March, 1995**

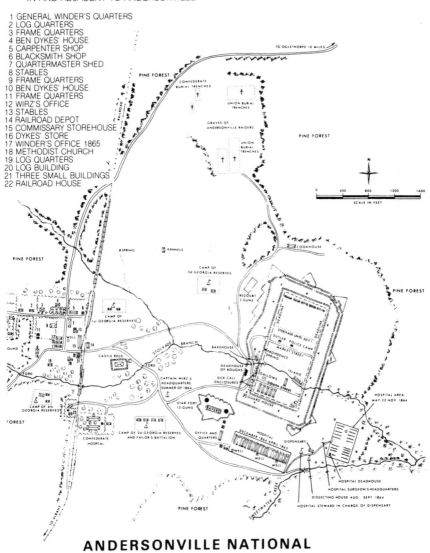

## KEY TO BUILDINGS
### IN AND ADJACENT TO ANDERSONVILLE

1 GENERAL WINDER'S QUARTERS
2 LOG QUARTERS
3 FRAME QUARTERS
4 BEN DYKES' HOUSE
5 CARPENTER SHOP
6 BLACKSMITH SHOP
7 QUARTERMASTER SHED
8 STABLES
9 FRAME QUARTERS
10 BEN DYKES' HOUSE
11 FRAME QUARTERS
12 WIRZ'S OFFICE
13 STABLES
14 RAILROAD DEPOT
15 COMMISSARY STOREHOUSE
16 DYKES' STORE
17 WINDER'S OFFICE 1865
18 METHODIST CHURCH
19 LOG QUARTERS
20 LOG BUILDING
21 THREE SMALL BUILDINGS
22 RAILROAD HOUSE

# ANDERSONVILLE NATIONAL
# HISTORIC SITE

*The following is the original frontispiece and 1865 preface to the Forbes Diary.*

# DIARY

OF

# A SOLDIER,

AND

# PRISONER OF WAR IN THE REBEL PRISONS.

---

WRITTEN BY EUGENE FORBES,
SERGEANT COMPANY B, 4TH REGIMENT NEW JERSEY VOLUNTEERS.

---

TRENTON:
MURPHY & BECHTEL, PRINTERS.

1865.

# PREFACE.

This book is precisely what is professed in its title, "The Diary of a Soldier." It was written by EUGENE FORBES, who served in the Volunteer Army from the commencement of the war until his death, at Florence, South Carolina, on the 7th of February, 1865. He was a native of Trenton, and served an apprenticeship with Messrs. Phillips & Boswell to the printing business. Subsequently, he was employed in the printing offices of Trenton, and at other places, until the call for troops to suppress the rebellion, issued by President Lincoln, on the 16th of April, 1861. Mr. Forbes was one of the first to respond to the call, abandoning his business to take up a rifle in defence of the Union. He entered the service from the purest motives; he was not stimulated by ambition, nor moved by a love of adventure, nor tempted by a large bounty. Believing the rebellion to be a criminal assault upon Republican Government, and its success the destruction of the Union of the States, he took up arms to suppress and punish rebellion, and preserve the Constitution and Union. He entered the Third Regiment of Militia, and served the three months for which he had enlisted. He returned to Trenton, and was mustered out in August, 1861, and immediately enlisted for three years in the Fourth Regiment, New Jersey Volunteers. With this regiment he joined the army of the Potomac, and after remaining in the vicinity of Alexandria until April, 1862, went with the rest of the regiment to the Peninsula. Here the regiment took part in all the engagements and marches of the army up to the battle of Gaines' Mills, where—after a gallant resistance—they were surrounded and captured. After a long and tedious imprisonment, they were exchanged, and Mr. Forbes returned to his duty, and shared in all the toils and battles of the Army of the Potomac until January, 1864. Then he, in company with some hundreds of his comrades, re-enlisted for another term of "three years or the war."

# PREFACE.

The Diary commences with the 1st of May, 1864, the opening of Grant's great campaign, commencing with the battles of the Wilderness, to end only with the fall of Richmond, and the surrender of Lee's army.

It will be sufficiently apparent that it was not written with a view to publication, but simply to occupy the idle hours of camp-life, and intended only for the inspection of the friends of the writer. There is, therefore, nothing for effect, and nothing disguised, but the plain statement of facts and occurrences as they presented themselves to the view of the writer. Related in this simple, unpretending style, the narrative of the sufferings of the Union prisoners in the rebel prisons, is peculiarly affecting, and we also come to understand the cause of the systematic ill treatment, the starving, the freezing and the shooting of our soldiers at the hands of the rebel authorities. It was to force them to enter the ranks of the rebel army; and this inhuman system succeeded in thousands of cases. There is a limit to human endurance, and after months of exposure, with an allowance of unwholesome food scarcely sufficient to sustain life, the spirit of thousands of prisoners became so broken that they were willing to even perjure themselves and turn traitors to escape the torture that the hellish ingenuity of the rebel jailors inflicted upon them.

The writer of this Diary was not one of these. Although of delicate constitution, and frequently suffering from ill health, he resisted all the torments his persecutors could inflict, and all the promises they could make—preferring to die in the line of his duty, to preserving life at the expense of honor. With those who knew him this will occasion no surprise, for they knew his unflinching courage and his unbending patriotism. To those who knew nothing of him, the Diary will still prove interesting, as a plain and unpretending narrative of painful suffering endured in a manly and uncomplaining spirit. The tortures of the rebel prison were borne by this brave man without flinching, even after his always feeble health had utterly broken down, until at last he was relieved by death. He died, as he had lived, in the faithful discharge of his duty, and his memory will be cherished by all who knew him, and all who can respect patriotism, courage, truth and fidelity

# MAY

Sunday, May 1. No news; the Hussars reported at Warrenton.*

Monday, May 2. The 2d Brigade shifted camp to this side of the river; Brigade parade A.M., and a man drummed out; heavy wind and rain storm P.M.; the picket line changed.

Tuesday, May 3. Pickets came in A.M.; dress parade P.M. Orders read announcing an advance, and exhorting every man to do his duty.

Wednesday, May 4. Aroused 3 A.M. and started 4 A.M.; reached Germanna Ford about 2 P.M., crossed the Rapidan on pontoon bridge and marched some two or three miles beyond it; very hot and dusty; my knapsack was carried with Capt. [Robert S.] Johnston's baggage; I carried two pieces of tent; got sick, tired, &c., but was told to take my time and do the best I could, and succeeded in joining regiment before it bivouacked. No mail. No enemy heard from.

Thursday, May 5. Roused about 4 A.M., and marched through the woods for some hours. About 10 A.M. Co. B.

*The 3rd New Jersey Cavalry was also known as the 1st U.S. Hussars.--Foster.

deployed as skirmishers; relieved about noon. Rebels attempted a flank movement, which we checked by charging and driving them back. Took 65 Georgians. [John H.] Richards, [John W.] Morris and [William] Wheaton wounded. Formed line again and made three more charges; "retired" once in a devil of a hurry, without any apparent cause. Slept in line of battle all night; three alarms. [Benajah M.] Plume, [John E.] McGannon, [David] Polk, [Joseph] Harrington, [Edward] Wilson and [William] Buckman wounded. My right foot very sore, the skin being all worn off the ball.

*(Continued at Andersonville.)* The regiment was in action at or near the right of the line. About noon our skirmishes were relieved, and the regiment remained quiet in line till about 4 or 5 P.M., when an aid-de-camp came riding in on our right flank and ordered the Colonel [Charles Ewing] to march us farther to the right; the Colonel did so. Firing was heard in front, and federal skirmishers, belonging to a Maine regiment, came in crying that the rebels were charging. Bullets were whistling lively around. The men by this time had commenced firing on the advancing rebs, who supposed they had a sure thing of it. The Colonel gave the order "Charge fix bayonets charge bayonets double quick march!" and we went in with a yell that told the men were eager for the fray. We charged some 400 to 500 yards, when *somebody* gave the order to halt and dress on the colors; some of the men had got 30 or 40 yards in advance of the regiment. I was ordered before the fight to take the Major's horse to the rear, but kept shady until I saw another fellow lead him off, and then rejoined the company. Wheaton, I believe, was the first man wounded; he was shot through the thigh; Morris was after water when the charge

commenced, and was wounded in the hand or arm, all so badly that amputation was necessary; Harrington is slightly wounded in the lip. We retired some 200 yards and made three more charges we lost McGannon, supposed mortally wounded, and Plume ditto; Polk slightly wounded; Buckman absent, and reported slightly wounded by the premature discharge of his gun while in the act of fixing or unfixing his bayonet. We laid in line of battle, without relief or support, all night. Three alarms, none of which amounted to anything. The loss of the regiment to-day was about 80 killed, wounded and missing. Shortly after the first charge an order was read from General [John] Sedgwick, complimenting the regiment for its bravery and services.

Friday, May 6. Roused at 4 A.M. and formed line of battle. Advanced some distance, then fell back to our old position. The rebels threw a few shells into the swamp, and it was quickly evacuated. The firing lasted about half an hour; after it ceased, we were moved further to the left, where we found part of the brigade. We now had an opportunity of making coffee, and getting something to eat, which we had not had since yesterday morning. About 4 P.M. we commenced building breastworks out of old logs, covering them with earth. We also buried a few secesh. After finishing the breastworks we were placed in the first line, lying behind the breastworks. The Major [David Vickers] had been in command all day, working like a Trojan, with Capt. Johnston acting as Major. The Colonel now appeared and took command.* After lying quiet for about half an hour, we were ordered by General [Thomas H. Neill] Neal (under whose command we had been placed,) to take post in the

*Col. Ewing was later charged with misbehavior before the enemy, stating that he, "did absent himself from his regiment , when they were moving forward, and engaging the enemy, and did not rejoin his regiment, until after it had gained the position indicated for them to occupy."--Service record.

the third and rear line, which we did, thus disappointing the
boys, who thought they were going to have "one pop" at
secesh from a "good posish." Toward dark firing
commenced on the right and rear; in a few minutes our
brigade was ordered to file right and take a position parallel
with the road on the left, to stop the runaways; but by some
misunderstanding, the regiment was taken out on the road
and marched past the Corps Headquarters, turning there to
the right, and digging out as fast as they could travel. The
panic became communicated to nearly the whole body of
troops, and all but about a regiment left the ground.
Generals Sedgwick, [Truman] Seymour and [Alexander]
Shaler used their utmost endeavors to stop the frightened
fugitives, but could only succeed in gathering about 1,000
fighting men. Among them I saw Capt. Johnston, the only
commissioned officer from our regiment, with a rifle, firing
and loading as rapidly as he could. Of the company, Corp.
[Hugh] McLaughlin was the only one I saw. We were all
three near the headquarters, in the road leading from the
breastworks to the main road. The tears were rolling down
Sedgwick's face, as he tried to rally the men, crying
"Shame! Shame!" but it was of no avail. A sergeant of our
regiment, who was formerly in the drum corps, and was
transferred to the ranks at his own request, was fighting by
my side, and fell shot through the body. His cries attracted
my attention, and at the same time I noticed that the Captain
and McLaughlin had disappeared. Things were getting
mighty hot, and as I saw the rebs gradually gaining ground
towards the headquarters, I thought I would get out before
they gained the road. Turning to the left, I had taken but a
few steps when I found their line already in possession of the
road, and between me and the headquarters. I fired my

piece into them (they were not thirty feet from me), and, without waiting to reload, dashed into the thick underbrush on the other side of the road running in front of the headquarters. A volley was sent after me, but never touched me.

**A post-war photograph taken in the Wilderness, near where Forbes was captured.**

"Digging out" to the best of my ability, I had run about 100 yards, when I ran plump into another line of them running parallel with the road, and was saluted with "Throw down that gun, Yank, you're surrounded." I "gin up", and was marched in rear of our breastworks, passing the sergeant before mentioned, turning the right of our works, and going along the whole line of rebel works, which were almost entirely deserted. After going some three miles we reached the turnpike. Before that we (some half dozen) were incorporated with another squad, among whom I found [Alfred] Hoffman and [Samuel Oakley] Bellerjeau, and some few others of the regiment. We were marched to Robinson's Tavern, some five or six miles, and placed under guard. There were from 800 to 1000 prisoners here, some of whom had been taken yesterday. Hoffman had been slightly wounded in the head. A colonel who had started with us, was wounded so badly that he had to be stopped and taken care of. Gen. Seymour was taken prisoner and accompanied us, together with some other officers. The rebs. were highly jubilant. Our captors were Georgians, who, it seems, we take, and who take us in regular turn. Oakley (Bellerjeau) had a narrow escape; a bullet struck him in the breast, entirely cutting through his coat, memorandum book, and was turned aside by his scissors, which he fortunately had in his pocket. How Capt. Johnston and McLaughlin escaped I do not know, but suppose they turned to the right and followed the line of breastworks, instead of turning to the left and trying to gain the road, as I did. But they got clear, and I am glad of it. The Major was taken prisoner, escaped and was again captured. Our loss foots up, so far as I know, as follows: Private [Patrick] Curran, killed; Private [John H.] Wood, wounded in the arm; Serg't Hoffman, wounded in head and taken; Serg't Forbes, taken prisoner. Robinson's Tavern is situated on the plank road, and is on the line we occupied last fall, at the time of the advance on Mine Run. [Lt.Gen. James] Longstreet's corps are all along the plank road, for some 3 miles, and the rebels have evidently a strong force here. I know nothing of the probable loss of the regiment in to-day's fight. A rebel soldier at the Tavern stole the hat from the head of one of our men, but no other property was taken from us. I picked up a shelter tent on the field, having lost my blanket. Very tired and foot-sore. The rebs say it will now be a race for Fredericksburg Heights.

Saturday, May 7. Marched to Orange Court House; at night taken on cars to Gordonsville; feet very sore, sold my rubber blanket for $2, and bought tobacco.

Sunday, May 8.   Left Gordonsville about 2 P.M. for Lynchburg; passed through Charlottesville, the prettiest place I have seen in Virginia; The town turned out *en masse* to see the captured "Yanks;" grades so steep that half of us were left for the night some miles beyond Charlottesville; very hot; some of the men searched at Gordonsville, and their watches, money, pocket knives, &c., taken from them.

Monday, May 9.   Started about 10 A.M. and reached Lynchburg about 5 P.M.; found some 1200 or 1500 Yank prisoners at the camp, which is in a deep ravine near the town; divided into squads and placed under sergeants, for the purpose of drawing rations, &c.; cloudy; Sergeant [Reynolds] Atwood, 108 N.Y., Co. E, has charge of our squad; Hoffman traded for some corn bread, so we have not suffered; we have no reliable news, but plenty of rumors; are guarded by militia and invalids; water is plenty, and, so far, we cannot complain.

Tuesday, May 10. Another squad (about 600) arrived to-day; some Jerseymen in it. Drew rations about noon, 5 crackers and a piece of bacon to each man; better crackers than Uncle Sam's, and the best bacon I have ever eaten. Traded my watch for two woolen blankets, so now we can keep warm. Party of ladies came down to look at the "Yanks", and some of the men behaved like fools. Rigged up a tent out of two of our blankets, and filled up one end with brush.

Wednesday, May 11. Wrote to Chris. (Larzelere,) in care of Capt. [William H.] Hatch, A. Adj. of Exchange[C.S.A.]; hope it will go. Drew rations at night, soft bread, ham, rice and salt. Rainy P.M., continuing all night; an orderly sergeant taken away; saw Dick Wardel; he was taken on Friday.

Thursday, May 12. Showery all day; men engaged in cutting a path for guards on the other side of the creek. Two men very sick in hospital, one with rupture, the other with typhoid fever. The wounded are generally doing well; a hospital tent has been erected, and a surgeon visits the camp daily. Men are generally in good spirits. Drew rations at night; soft bread, (back rations,) hard bread, rice, salt, and bacon; a good ration, and enough, if it continues. Rainy all night. Reported that we are to be sent away tomorrow.

Friday, May 13. One week since we were taken. Another squad of prisoners came in, (some 100.) Started about noon, during a heavy shower, for some place unknown, supposed to be Danville; traveled slow, passing several towns and villages, one of which (Farmville)? contained several hospitals. We are in good passenger cars and not much crowded. Some of the Farmville ladies shook their little fists at us, and one waved her bloomer. "Bully" for her.

Saturday, May 14. Thirty-one years old today, and a prisoner. Still on the road; the guards in charge do all they can for our comfort. Arrived at Danville about 3 P.M., and were quartered in an old tobacco warehouse; never been used as a prison before. Some of the citizens distributed bread freely along the line, every one was civil, and I did not hear an insult offered to any of our men. A sergeant appointed over each floor, and the men divided into squads of twenty. Reported we are to go to Georgia; it takes ten days for the trip. Drew rations in Danville; half loaf of corn bread, and a small piece of bacon; the Quartermaster told us we would get soup tomorrow; the bread is sufficient for three meals. A man was struck by a sentry for crowding him, but not seriously injured. Rainy all night.

Sunday, May 15. Rations served out P.M.; bread pork and rice soup plenty. Our P.O. address is Danville prison, No. 5, 1st floor. Rainy today. Got the headache from the confounded noise.

Monday, May 16. Rations about noon, same as yesterday. One man found, having his name on the squad roll. Quite an excitement apparently in the town; militia marching, &c. Sentry fired at some one last night in rear part of building; no one hurt; another shot first this morning, with same result. Rainy A.M. but cleared up P.M.

Tuesday, May 17. Rations about noon; bacon and bread. 399 men on this floor; about 1,100 in the building. Sent a letter to McKenzie. Several wounded and sick men here, but no surgeon to attend them. Drew bean soup P.M. Clear and warm. Sick and wounded men taken away during the afternoon; many of the men afflicted with the diarrhea.

Wednesday, May 18. Drew two days' rations today. A number of convalescents came in from hospital, some of them having been prisoners for eight months. Rainy P.M.

Thursday, May 19. Left Danville about seven A.M. by railroad for Greensboro'; traveled in cars some thirty-five or forty miles, then walked some four miles to a station; passed several trains with secesh soldiers returning from furlough; the boys traded freely with them, and the old feeling of personal animosity seems to have died out, except in a very few cases. Heard various rumors about the contending armies—that Grant had been forced back of the Rappahannock, with a loss of from forty-five to seventy thousand killed, wounded and missing; that [Maj.Gen. P.G.T.] Beauregard had defeated [Maj.Gen. Benjamin] Butler and [Maj.Gen. William F.] Smith, between Petersburg and Drury's Bluff, capturing some eight or nine thousand prisoners; in short, that we are beaten at all points; that [Maj.Gen. Nathaniel] Banks is surrounded in Louisiana, &c., &c. Stopped at the station till dark; about sundown two trains arrived; showery P.M., and about 11 P.M. we started, traveling all night.

Friday, May 20. Traveled all night, and kept on till about 6 P.M., when we arrived at Charlotte (ville?), N.C., and stopped for the night. Rations were issued to squads of 100 men; we got into a squad which turned out to have 114 men,

Atwood raised some bacon, Oakley sold his pocketbook for
five dollars (Confed.), and bought some biscuit, so we went
to bed full at last. A cavalry sergeant fell off the cars, and
is supposed to have been killed. Traded my gold pen for
some biscuit, last night. Clear. Wrote this by moonlight.
Laid down and slept soundly.

Saturday, May 21. Part of us (some 600) started off at 7
A.M.; we remained; traded my housewife and scissors for
ten biscuits; rigged an awning out of our blankets; traded
several small articles for biscuit; cooked our bacon, and
lounged about till about two P.M., when we got into box
cars, and got under way about four o'clock; a squad of
Union officers arrived before we started, and are in the same
train with us; saw Major [David] Vickers, of the 4th, and
Capt. [Henry Parkhurst Cooke] Cook, A. A. G..

**Maj. David Vickers (left), and Capt. H.P. Cook (right).**

The Major sent to know if we had any knowledge of officers of the brigade being killed or wounded; asked something about Capt. Johnston, which I could not understand; clear and warm; traveled all night; crossed one medium sized river, and passed through several very pretty towns; found out that the name of the place where we stayed last night is "Charlotte", without the "ville."

Sunday, May 22.    Arrived at Columbia, S. C., about sunrise; saw some very fine buildings in the place; country we have traveled through is generally wild and wooded, though with but small timber; stopped near Columbia some time, and saw Major Vickers; he knows nothing about Capt. Johnston; a few miles beyond Columbia we caught up to the advance squad, and changed cars; a quarter of a cupful of corn was issued to each man for coffee; passed several fine looking towns; traveled all night; passing through South Carolina, we saw the darkies all arrayed in their holiday attire, and in much larger numbers than we have previously seen them; divided our last two crackers about sundown; parched our corn and made quite a sumptuous repast; one door of the car closed at night; fifty-five men inside, and the air almost suffocating; very little sleep to be had, as there was not room for any man to lie down.

Monday, May 23. Arrived at Augusta, Ga., about daylight; goodly sized town; changed cars about seven A.M.; Oakley traded the buttons off his dress-coat for two large biscuit; he also sold my pipe for five dollars, (scrip,) and bought fifteen biscuit for the money; tarried at Augusta for some time, and drew three days' rations; three and a half large crackers, about half a pound of corn bread, and about three-quarters of a pound of ham or bacon. Some few of the men are terribly lousy already. Very warm. The old guard left us here, and we are now guarded by Georgians, who, like their soldiers in the field, seem to be the best and most reasonable of the Confederates I have met with. Traveled all night, and apparently at a faster rate than usual; got more sleep than on any previous night, but very warm and crowded; one door closed, as usual, and no one allowed on top of the car.

Tuesday, May 24. Arrived at Macon about daylight; medium sized town, of good appearance; found I was in company with several men of my own regiment, Company H. Arrived at Andersonville, Ga., about noon, and after considerable delay, were turned into a large enclosure, where we found about 15,000 prisoners, many of whom had been prisoners for nine and ten months. Trafficing in tent-poles, salt, corn bread, &c., was soon going on extensively;

**Prisoners being marched into Andersonville.**

some of the men are like skeletons, from chronic diarrhea, &c.; some are as black as charcoal men, and have evidently not washed for many days; they seem to have lost all ambition, and of the 15,000 now here, not one-half could march five miles; the camp is about six hundred yards long by four hundred wide, and surrounded by a high board fence, some twelve or fourteen feet high, with two gates on the west side; sentry boxes are placed at regular intervals along the wall. Drew rations of corn bread and bacon at dark.

Wednesday, May 25. Roll-call about 9 A.M.; a heavy shower last night; our squad is Detachment 57, Mess 1; washed ourselves and our clothes the first time since our capture. Gambling is carried on quite extensively; faro, sweat-cloths, dice, &c., are used, and $10 stakes are played for, as if money was as plenty as sand. Six men were carried out on the "dead line" last night from our (the south) side of the camp. A considerable marsh occupies the very center of the pen, which, if not drained, will be apt to create disease among us; the drinking water is very poor; wells are dug, and kept as private property, but the rebel surgeon says the running water is the most wholesome; we use the run water altogether; the well water appears impregnated with sulphur, or some mineral, looks blue, and induces diarrhea. A large squad of prisoners from the western army arrived this P.M.; they report that Gen. Joseph Johnston has been taken prisoner by Sherman. One of the old prisoners states that the deaths here in the last two months will reach 1,800. Trade is carried on with the guards on the outside of the wall, by talking through cracks, and throwing articles over the fence. Rigged up our tent anew, and commenced a regular "skirmish drill;" took no prisoners, but counted about a dozen dead on the field (my shirt). Several negroes are here, captured in Florida; a negro orderly sergeant has charge of a squad of whites and blacks; the negroes are treated in all respects like ourselves; several Indians are also here, so we make a motley crew. Drew rations towards night, corn bread, bacon, and boiled rice. Sentry fired a shot just after dark, but believe no one was hurt; some of our men came in with the squad which arrived this evening, and more are expected tomorrow; they report that only eighty men are left for duty in the regiment, and that Grant's headquarters are twenty-two miles from Richmond.

Thursday, May 26. "Skirmished," as usual. A party of negroes were set at work digging for tunnels, the existence of which is most probably only in the imaginations of the guards; the officer in charge says he will look no more, but give us a ration of grape and canister if an attempt to escape is made. Two men who were with me in the three months' service, came to see me last night (Louis and Kelly); they have been prisoners about four months, but look very well; Louis is now in the cavalry, and Kelly in the gunboat service. Reported that one man was killed and another wounded last night; various rumors afloat in regard to paroling, &c., but none of which the slightest reliance can be placed. Peddling still goes on; a "bunch" (two little onions,) for 25 cents; a 10 cent plug of tobacco, 50 cents and so on. Some of the dirtiest men were ducked and scrubbed today, and some of the "raiders" (thieves), bucked and gagged, and their heads shaved. The weather is warm, with frequent showers. Boxes and letters are received here by the prisoners. Drew pork and mush at dark, but no bread. A squad of prisoners arrived after dark, some of the 4th among them, who report the regiment reduced to eighty effective men.

Friday, May 27. A "raider" caught last night, and kept prisoner till daylight, when he was bucked and gagged, his head shaved, and afterwards marched around the camp; he took it very coolly. A fight occurred between a party of "raiders" and some of the "raidees", in which the latter got the worst of it; one man is said to be pretty badly hurt. Quite an excitement is apparent among the guards outside; the infantry are marching to various points, and horsemen carrying messages from one body to another. One tunnel was discovered yesterday, and the existence of others is probably suspected. Very hot, and the odor from the swamp and sinks by no means pleasant. Three tunnels discovered today, one said to extend sixty feet beyond the stockade. Drew bread, rice and meat about 8 P.M.; the ration appears to be getting smaller by degrees. Tore out the sleeve and back linings of my blouse, cut up our sugar and coffee bags, and cut off the flap of Hoffman's knapsack, sewed them together, and made an end for the tent. A prisoner who came in night before last reports Lieuts. [David] Flannery and [Joseph] Heston captured on the 13th.

Saturday, May 28. A considerable number of prisoners arrived from Atlanta this morning. Artillery was distinctly heard this morning. Report states that Atlanta is now in possession of our troops; some of Sherman's scouts are said to have been taken this side of it, and are now in here. Drew bread, bacon, and mush and rice mixed, P.M. Surgeons attend the sick regularly; the sick are taken outside the gate to be prescribed for. They are strengthening the palisades by clamping them with iron clamps. Made up our minds that we must get along on two meals a day. Weather very warm.

Sunday, May 29. A squad of about 900 prisoners arrived today; among them is [William] Jagers, also [Thomas] Mulvaney; [John] Duncan is wounded and taken; [Abner] Gaskill is reported killed; Col. Ewing mortally wounded; [Andrew] Broughton supposed killed; the regiment reduced to 75 or 80 effective men.* The Ninth Army Corps is now represented in the camp. Dick Wardell, of the 6th Regiment, arrived here today; he is the Orderly Sergeant who was imprisoned at Richmond, and has but lately been released. There are now about 17,000 men in this camp. Drew bread, rice and bacon P.M., earlier than we have drawn before. Very warm. Jagers says that Capt. Johnston is wounded; they were taken on the 12th, near Spottsylvania Court House; he says our cavalry entered Gordonsville four hours after they left it, and destroyed the warehouses; that Petersburg is in our hands, &c.; all "camp talk," of course, but probably with a few grains of truth in it. A party of Yanks went outside to work, but declined building a new stockade.

Monday, May 30. Boiled our last night's ration of rice with corn bread and bacon, making a sort of soup; eating but two meals per day, but do not suffer from hunger; breakfast about 8 A.M., and supper about 3 P.M. After dinner got Oak. spinning twisters, and talking about "spuds," "corn beef," "duffs," &c., until we all got as hungry as blazes.

*See Appendix III, page 191.

The markets are very brisk: black beans, 40c. per pint; corn bread, 40c. per loaf; a small armful of wood (pine), 25 to 50c.; a set of tent poles, from $1 to $4; eggs, $2.50 to $4 per dozen; tobacco, from 75c. to $1.25 per small plug; dried peas, 40c. per pint; dried apples, ; soap, from 25c to 75c per piece 2½ inches square; blankets, from $5 to $20; razors, from $3 to $5, a shave, 10c. We are using soap-stone as soap, and some of the men use it for washing their clothes. They are still clamping the stockade. A squad of about 400 prisoners arrived today, taken on the 16th inst.; they report our army repulsed three times from Fort Darling, but still besieging the place; that Grant has been reinforced by 60,000 men; that the Sixth Corps has been relieved by the 22d Corps, and sent to the left, &c., &c. Oak and myself have gone on short allowance of tobacco for some days, and estimate that we can stick it out for three weeks yet; I have 2½ ten cent plugs, not quite as much as I would generally use in one week. Sherman reported to be falling back from Atlanta, 170 miles distant. Had quite a "jaw" with Jagers and Mulvaney; one says [John] Duncan is wounded, and the other denies it; [Charles H.] Hagerman is not wounded; [John] Hindley reported wounded. Drew rations about dark; they are growing "smaller by degrees, and beautifully less;" one-third of a loaf of bread, and a piece of bacon about the size of a penny sponge-cake, one tablespoonful of mush. A rebel colonel was in camp today, and told some of the boys that we would not be here two weeks longer; that hereafter we should have full rations whether they could cook it or not, &c., &c. New sinks are being built, and the camp otherwise improved.

Tuesday, May 31. A detail of 18 men and a sergeant to cut wood to cook rations. About three-fourths of a loaf of bread were drawn by squads up to 27, the rest of us drew dry corn meal; so it seems the colonel is making some improvement. He stated this A.M. that he did not wish the men to be depressed or elated by stories from the outside regarding paroling, exchanging, &c.; that the arrangements for exchanging and parole were perfected, but could not be carried out until the Virginia campaign was terminated; but as soon as there was a cessation of active hostilities, part of the men would be exchanged, and the remainder paroled *all* would be released. This sounds very fair, and has more or less effect on the minds of every one, and the colonel being seemingly a frank, openhearted man, it may be true; but to one who remembers the experience of Belle Isle, and the various statements made by generous, kind-mannered officers of the rebel persuasion thereon, coupled with the knowledge that desperate attempts at escape have been made from here, it fails to dispel a suspicion that it may be a story invented to quiet the men, and induce them to abandon, for the future, all such attempts. "time will tell." With Grant thundering at the gates of Richmond, and Sherman (as per rumor) demanding the surrender of Atlanta, we can afford to wait quietly the "course of events," so long as the grub is not cut too short. A company of prisoners from Florida arrived today; they were on picket when captured, the remainder of the regiment being on a foray for beef. We got two medium-sized sticks of wood for 30 men; our "splitting tools" are of the most primitive kind, the only iron instruments being an army table knife and a railroad spike. We drew a pint of meal to each man, with salt sufficient to cook it; baked a few of the cakes to try my hand. Sherman reported to have entered Atlanta, with a loss of 15,000 men. The deaths in hospital here are reported to range from 40 to 80 per day.

**Photograph taken by A.J. Riddle on August 16, 1864 showing the northwest area of the stockade and the sinks along Stockade Branch of Sweetwater Creek. Note the deadline in the lower right corner.**

# JUNE

Wednesday, June 1. Baked our breakfast, and liked our cakes better than the bread. Got up at 4 A.M., and took a walk around the camp; it is a deplorable sight at that hour in the morning; men scattered all around, many of them without other clothing or covering than a shirt and drawers; some in the last agonies of death; others writhing under the pangs of disease or wounds; some as black as mulattoes with smoke and dirt; and nearly all with signs of heart-weariness written on their faces. The first day of summer. Another squad of prisoners arrived today, some from Grant's army, and some from Sherman. Spent most of the morning baking corn bread. Heavy rain storm came on, drenching everything, running through the tents, quenching the fires, and nearly drowning the poor fellows down in the lowlands. Reported that we are to be sent to Savannah, in squads of 1,000 men, commencing on Monday next. Duncan is here, in a squad on the north side; he is wounded in the back. About 34 men of the regiment are prisoners, nearly or quite all in good health; Hoffman, Jagers, Mulvaney, Duncan and Forbes, Co. B. Drew corn meal and bacon P.M.; got some wood. Some of the 9th New Jersey came in today; Mat. Hill among them; they are very much down on Butler. A rebel paper

(*Atlanta Intelligencer*) states that all prisoners taken up to the 7th May are to be exchanged; this would just save my bacon, being taken on the 6th; it also states that the United States claim to have a surplus of some 33,000 prisoners. It reports a fierce contest as raging at "Church Hill," near Atlanta, on May 28th, the result of which was not decided at the time of publication. Our soap is all used up, and our clothes are becoming the color of coffee grounds remarkably fast. Cloudy all night.

Thursday, June 2. Drew meal and bacon, but no salt. Rice is selling at 60 cts. per pint here. Thunder showers all around us, but none here. A very dull day, and very few rumors floating about. Attempted to wash my shirt and drawers without soap, but it was impossible to obtain even an appearance of cleanness; the pitch-pine smoke sticks to both clothes and men like grease. Took a walk and looked for some of the 9th Regiment boys, but could not find them. A shot fired, but no one hurt. Our meal lasts much better than the bread did. Drew salt after dark. Heavy thunder showers came over about sundown, lasting till about 9 P.M. A spiritualist in camp, prophesying in regard to the war, stated that Richmond and Atlanta would both fall within a few days; that the war would suddenly cease, &c. Hope his predictions may be verified, but my faith is weak. Reported that some men escaped, as the dogs were out, and some excitement manifested outside.

Friday, June 3. A fight before roll-call; one man against four, but no one seriously injured. Saving five grains of Columbia corn (S.C.) to plant if I ever get home. Played draughts, took a walk on the other side, mailed a letter for

Louis Traute, got some paper and envelopes from Jagers, and tried every conceivable plan to kill time. A squad of prisoners came in P.M. some of them captured on the 19th ult. They report Grant at Hanover Junction and Mechanicsville, throwing up entrenchments. While I write, some of our men are at work for the rebels, throwing up fortifications over the railroad, thus forging their own chains. Two rebel citizens visited the camp today, when the usual badinage occurred between them and some of the prisoners. Four weeks a prisoner today, and in good health and spirits. Drew meal, salt and bacon after dark. The number of prisoners who arrived today is 517. There are now about 21,000 here. The deaths in hospital are reported to average about 60 per day. Rainy after 5 P.M. all night.

Saturday, June 4. Rainy all day. Cooked dumplings, made out of corn meal, by way of change, and found them very palatable. Several prisoners who escaped from here some 12 days ago were brought in, having been recaptured; they all have balls and chains; there must be now nearly 100 men wearing these articles. Some prisoners from Sherman's army were also brought in, taken a week ago; they report four days' hard fighting 30 miles from Atlanta. Drew meal, beans, salt and bacon P.M. Symptoms of diarrhea.

Sunday, June 5. A 2d New Jersey prisoner, captured on the 14th May, reports [Duncan] McKenzie as missing; hope he is not hurt; also, that Capt. Johnston was slightly wounded.* Wrote a short note to mother. Showery A.M. Cooked our beans. Drew cooked rations P.M., mush, beans (so sour that we threw them away), bread and bacon. We have gained on our rations until we now have a whole day's ration of meal

*Captain Robert S. Johnston received a slight head wound at Spotsylvania. -Service record.

ahead, but meat is a scarce article. Some of the men received boxes from home yesterday. Showery A.M., but cleared up P.M.

Monday, June 6. Cloudy and misty at day break, but cleared up at sunrise; showery P.M.; just one month since we were captured. Drew bread and bacon P.M. The enlargement of the enclosed area still goes on; seven acres are to be added, making 17 in all, some three and a half or four of which are occupied by a swamp, which is well calculated to breed fevers this summer. The stockades over the brook are ingeniously arranged, so as to catch all the filth which is swept down during rain storms, and leave it in this swamp, thus adding to the highly (if not pleasantly) perfumed odor of the "pen;" as A. Ward would say, "this is meant for a *goak*." Deaths in hospital for 24 hours ending at 12 last night, reported to be 98—"I gather them in." One of the surgeons says, 8,000 new prisoners are to come as soon as the new stockade is finished—"first catch your hare." Lively skirmishing today; caught and killed 17 or 20 lice, all fat and in good condition. Atwood traded off 50 cents worth of stamps for soap, and we all had the luxury of a good wash all over; notice one peculiarity in washing clothes here, you can always catch more lice on them *after* being washed, than before, so I judge the run is well populated. People at home generally take off their boots and clothes on going to bed, and put them on in the morning; we reverse the custom, take them off in the morning, and replace them at night.

Tuesday, June 7. Went over and saw Duncan; his feet are very much swollen with inflammatory rheumatism; a man was bucked and gagged this A.M. for striking his tent-mate with a club, knocking him senseless. 87 deaths reported in hospital up to 12 last night. Rumor says Fort Darling is captured. Very hot. Some 500 or 600 prisoners came in after noon, most of whom have been prisoners some time; the crew of a war vessel were brought in, their craft being surprised at night, off Savannah, only four men being on the lookout; the prisoners say that the railroad bridge at Danville was destroyed four hours after they left that place, by our calvary. Walked around and looked at the little gardens the men have planted around some of their tents; none are more than three inches wide, extending around three sides of the tent, and beans and corn planted therein. Grant is reported within four miles of Richmond; the sailors of the "Water Witch" report that they killed seven and wounded seventeen of the rebels, losing only one of their number.* Drew bread and bacon P.M. Serg't [John] Foster, of Company "K", and some five or six others, came in today; he says McKenzie is wounded or missing, Ewing killed, Johnston wounded, the brigade broken up, consolidated with the Second Brigade, and under the command of Col. [Emory] Upton. Rainy P.M., lasting all night.

Wednesday, June 8. Serg't Foster dropped in to see us; he says Gaskill and Robert Pierson were killed at Spottsylvania, on May 12; that Capt. [Samuel] Gaul was in command of the regiment; that [Hugh] McLaughlin is in charge of the company; that Hoffman is reported killed, and I reported wounded and captured; that [Lt. Harrison A.] Skillman has rejoined the regiment, and Lew. Dowerty is dead; Foster was

*The Water Witch was captured near Savannah on June 2nd.

taken near the North Anna River, some twenty miles from Richmond, on the 24th May. He says the hardest fighting, according to rebel accounts, has been since his capture, and they acknowledge Grant to be holding his own. He also says that a recruit from Co. B came in with him, but did not know his name. Fixed our tent anew, something like a wall tent; heretofore it has resembled a wagon cover. Cloudy all the morning, but cleared up hot P.M. A squad of prisoners came in P.M.; some of them were captured as late as the 4th inst.; they are like Absalom's men, for they "know not anything." Drew one-third loaf of bread, rice (raw), and bacon P.M. Letters were delivered to the prisoners today. All sorts of rumors are flying about camp relative to paroling, exchanging, &c., but nothing reliable. The stockade is very much crowded, there being over 23,000 prisoners here. Three fights today.

Thursday, June 9. 127 deaths reported in hospital up to 12 o'clock last night. Two or three died today just after being carried out to the Doctors. A negro died inside this A.M. The "raiders" held high festival last night; one man was wakened by them, and found the edge of a knife across his throat, and was told that death was his portion if he uttered a cry; they relieved him of a blanket and some money; the mark of the knife was still on his throat this morning. Onions and turnips, of a medium size, are selling at one dollar apiece. Chris ought to have a stall down here. Heavy showers after dinner. Cooked some of our rice, with meat and dumplings, making a very palatable soup: "All the labor of man is for his mouth." Some of the "wood squads" have been escaping, so this morning an order was read, that no men should be allowed out without first pledging themselves not to attempt to escape; should men escape after taking this "parole" the mess they belong to is to receive rations only on every other day until they are recaptured; the sergeants of messes are to accompany the men, on parole. Two ministers of the Gospel were here this morning; they stated that Grant had closely invested Richmond, being within four miles of the city, and that there was no probability of exchange or parole for some time. Pepper 25 cts. per spoonful. Drew meal, salt and bacon P.M. More heavy showers towards night. Several shots fired after nightfall, but no word of any one being injured.

Friday, June 10. Five weeks a prisoner. Hoffman very sick, this morning, with a heavy fever. The scarlet fever is said to prevail here extensively. Very hot this morning. Chief rumor of the day is, that we are to be sent away on parole, commencing on the 15th inst; "big thing wish I could see it." Get up every morning at four o'clock now, and generally take a nap in the heat of the day. Had my hair cut so short, yesterday, that Oak says I look like a Chinese Mandarin; John Wood, Co. D, 97th N.Y.C., cut it. Made rice soup out of bones, &c. Atlanta again reported to be occupied by Sherman forces. Drew meal, bacon and salt P.M. Shower P.M.

Saturday, June 11. Baking soda 25 cts. per tablespoonful; molasses, 75 cts. per half pint. The sergeant of 62d Detachment has received a letter from his captain (now at Macon) stating that arrangements are perfected for an exchange at the close of the present campaign. Hoffman better. A speculator, selling sugar at 25 cts. per spoonful, was set upon, beaten by the raiders, and his sugar taken, after a hard struggle. Very hot until about five P.M., when it commenced raining. Drew yellow meal, salt and bacon. Grant reported to have fallen back six miles from Richmond; Sigel reported to have been driven back on Winchester.

Sunday, June 12. Atwood borrowed a "sifter" and sifted our corn meal; large quantity of chaff, which we scorch and use for coffee. Mat Hill came to see us; says [Capt. James Madison] Mad Drake is a prisoner; [James] Pip (Houghtaling) is safe; is very much down on Butler, who, he says, has been removed.* Rainy P.M. A squad of prisoners came in, mostly from Sherman's army; some few from Grant, who report no fighting beyond skirmishing. A very strong rumor prevails that paroling has commenced; It is stated that the officers have been sent from Macon to Savannah; some of the prisoners who came in today say they saw them getting into the cars. Gen. [John H.] Winder is said to be coming to take command of the forces and prisoners here. One of the surgeons told Atwood, some days ago, that our rations would soon be reduced in quantity. Our receiving *thirty-nine* quarts of rice, and thirty-six pounds of bacon, without bread or meal, as one day's ration for two hundred and ninety men, proves his assertion to be true, and leads us to believe the rebel quartermaster's remark, that "the Southern Confederacy is about played out." Hope the Belle Island allowance will not be established permanently here. Rain continued all night.

*Capt. James Madison Drake, of Co. K, 9th New Jersey Infantry was captured at Drewry's Bluff, Va., on May 16th. He was first confined in Libby Prison, and later transferred to Macon and then to Savannah, then to Charleston. While being transferred to Columbia, Drake escaped and made his way to Federal lines at Knoxville. For this daring exploit, he was awarded the Medal of Honor.--Deeds of Valor*

Monday, June 13. Rainy all day. Wheat flour has declined to 50c. per pint; salt, to 25c. per five spoonfuls; rice, 25c. per pint, butter, $4.50 per lb. Rumored that Sherman has cut communications, thus putting us on short allowance. No roll call. No medicine for several days. There are quite a number of insane men in camp; one of them has been plundered of everything but his shirt, and while he was asleep, some scoundrel cut off the front tail of that garment, thus leaving him almost without anything to cover his nakedness. Today and yesterday have been so cold that an overcoat would be a comfort, and he must suffer extremely; he was refused admission to the hospital today. Several of the old Belle Island prisoners were vaccinated, before leaving that place, with impure or scrofulous matter; some of these men have since had their arms amputated, while others are walking around with their bones and muscles exposed, the flesh having dropped out piecemeal. Lame men, blind men, deaf men, one-armed men, all alike exposed to the inclemency of the storm, or the blistering rays of the sun; "As ye do unto others it shall be done unto you, and with what measure ye mete, it shall be measured to you again." Drew rice, salt and bacon P.M. Some of the squads drew rice and molasses, but no bacon. Rain continued all night. A few prisoners came in; no news.

Tuesday, June 14. Rain continues. A few prisoners came in. Drew meal, bacon, salt and boiled rice. At about 11 P.M. a terrible row seemed to be taking place about the center of the camp; cries of murder and the sound of blows were heard, alarming the rebs so much that the sentries cried the time every half hour, instead of every hour, as usual. No squads allowed out for wood, two men having escaped yesterday. Last night no response was heard from seven sentry boxes, commencing at No. 17; this morning it was ascertained that fourteen of our men had "tunneled out," and that seven guards had accompanied them, taking their arms and accoutrements. Active skirmishing.

Wednesday, June 15. Saw one man laid out, who died from cold and exposure last night. On the north side they are riding one of the raiders on a rail. A large squad of prisoners came in this A.M., among whom are several from the 4th Regiment; [William] Cooper, of Co. B., is said to be among the number, and to have been captured on the 8th ult. They report that they could hear musketry as they left Libby Prison; they have heard nothing regarding parole or exchange. An individual who was getting a list of names of shoemakers who were willing to go outside and work for the benefit of the Southern Confederacy, was seized by some of the boys on the north side, bucked and gagged, his head shaved, his list taken away from him, and then turned loose, amid the hootings of the crowd. The Captain and Quartermaster told the Sergeant of 57-3 that paroles would be issued tomorrow up to the 20th Detachment. Bet he lies. Drew meal, salt, bacon and raw rice. No one allowed out for wood. Reported that Lincoln has been renominated by the Republicans, and [George B.] McClellan by the Democrats. Cooper says Grant has 16,000 prisoners in rear of Fredericksburg; First Battalion Veteran Reserve Corps reported ordered to the field. Rainy A.M., but cleared up P.M.

Thursday, June 16. Cloudy all day, with some little rain. Two squads on the north side were deprived of their rations, on account of their connection with the shaving of the shoemaker's head yesterday. (I believe his name is Kearney some of the raiders appear acquainted with him.) Drew meal and bacon. A large squad of prisoners (some 300) came in P.M.; they are mostly from the Army of the Potomac; they report desperate fighting; that Grant moves his picket line every evening close to the rebs, during the night moves his line of battle up to the picket line, throws up earthworks and mounts artillery, in the morning charges, &c. Some of these men were taken at Gaines' Mill, the scene of the Fourth's Capture in 1862. Fifty-seven deaths reported in hospital last night. Letters came for many of the men today. Of course the captain lied yesterday about the parole. One of the sailors lent Atwood a History of America, and it helps to pass time very pleasantly. Used my last chew of tobacco. Rained very hard after dark.

Friday, June 17. Rainy all day. Gen. Winder reported here.* Several men out on wood squads turned on the guard, took their guns, and made their escape. No more allowed out for wood. Drew meal and bacon P.M. Raiding is getting very extensively practiced. Six weeks prisoners today. Wood getting scarce.

Saturday, June 18. One man slept in the mush box last night; he was surrounded by five or six men during the night, and his pocket cut out; another, walking around with a blanket on his shoulders, was seized by four men, and his blanket taken away.

*Gen. John Winder, arrived on June 16th, and took command of Camp Sumter.

About 11 o'clock today a man was knocked down and robbed of his watch and $80. "Things is lovely." Rainy by spells. Atwood got tired of his job as commissary sergeant, and threw up the "sit." Some of the men who escaped yesterday were returned today; one of them was shot through the thigh, the other one's forehead was grazed. A squad of prisoners came in about noon, all from hospitals, wounded and sick. Atwood resigned, and Buckley accepted commissary sergeant. "Run." got some vinegar yesterday; it was the color of egg nog, and was made of some acid and water mixed. Potatoes $1.50 per dozen; about 16 fill a quart pot. More parole rumors, but without credibility. Went to see Mat. Hill; he lives near the "raiders." Showery all day, but with a promise of clearing.

Sunday, June 19. A rainbow this morning. A large black snake was seen by one of the men between the "dead line" and the stockade. He asked permission of the nearest guard to pass the line and kill it, which was given. A sentry on a distant post fired at the man killing the snake, missed him, but struck a tent, wounding two men, one in the head, and the other in the thigh. Some of the prisoners who came in yesterday were wounded as late as May 16th, and their arms, legs, &c. which have been amputated or otherwise acted upon, are perfectly raw. Last night a well, which had been dug very near some tents, caved in, burying three men, who slept in a tent near the edge of the well. Two of them were got out safely, but the third was injured so badly that he was dead by roll call. The camp was more quiet last night than any time since we have been in it. The rebel sergeant says that Gen. Winder is here. Atwood asserts that two of our men were to have been hung, by order of Capt. [Henry

Wirz] Wurtz, for over powering the guard, and that Gen. Winder gave orders that no such execution should take place. Some of the men who were in that party are now in camp, the General having forbidden the balls and chains to be put on them. They say that they wandered about that night, but there being no stars to guide their course, they become bewildered, and twice before daylight found themselves close to the stockade. So much for going without a map or compass. A large squad of prisoners came in on the north side this afternoon. Rainy all the afternoon. Our surplus meal has soured from the damp weather. Oak. traded a quart of it for a piece of tobacco. Drew meal, bacon and salt; got a bone for my ration, with more meat on it than on two ordinary rations. Rainy by spells all day. Drew wood.

Monday, June 20. Cloudy and drizzling A.M. No roll call this morning. Blackberries are selling at fifty cents a pint; green apples are in camp, but I did not price them. Washed my shirt, but did not get it dry. Traded two quarts of meal for a pint of beans, and tried to make some bean soup; rained all P.M. putting out our fire, and we had to eat our beans half cooked. Got the diarrhea very bad, may be raw beans will cure it. Had to sleep without my shirt.

Tuesday, June 21. Cleared up this morning. Find I will have to reduce my chirography to its fighting standard, as the book is getting pretty well filled up. Heavy rain P.M. Drew meal, salt and tainted bacon P.M. Went out to the Doctor in the morning, but did not get prescribed for. Saw a large number of men at the dead-house, so many that it would not hold them all, some fifteen or twenty being laid outside. Every one was searched on returning through the gate. Lost

nothing. A man was shot on or near the dead-line this P.M.
A raider caught stealing a frying pan near 12 P.M. Rumored
that Sherman has been defeated, and that Grant has fallen
back 14 miles; also, that Fort Darling has been captured for
the 999th time. No room in the hospital for more sick, a
large number lying outside now. A few prisoners came in.
Considerable excitement among the rebs, by a report that
[Maj.Gen. Judson] Kilpatrick is near here. Rebs drawn up
in line of battle all day and night. Hope he will come. No
roll call today. Squads still working on the stockade.

Wednesday, June 22. Clear this morning. All quiet.
Brown, of our detachment, has been shamefully treated by
some of the men. He has the chronic diarrhea, and having
met with an accident, washed his pants and drawers and hung
them up to dry. Some scoundrel stole them, leaving him
with nothing but a shirt. One of the men gave him a pair of
drawers, and he now lies near the runlet, his feet awfully
swollen and gradually sinking under disease. Our own men
are worse to each other than the rebels are to us. A tunnel
was discovered today, and the men ordered to dig it out and
then fill it up. The man who was shot last night reported
dead today. Saw two men carried out this morning from our
side. Louis Traute is very bad with scurvy and diarrhea, and
Jagers has the dysentery very bad. Gambling still goes on
very extensively, and *hundreds of dollars* are changing hands
daily. No roll call again this morning. Made a regular
dinner today; soup, dumplings, bread and coffee, all made of
Indian meal. Rumored that paroling is to commence between
the 7th and 17th July. A few sprinkles of rain in the
afternoon, just enough to maintain the reputation of the
month. Drew meal, salt and bacon P.M. Cucumbers in

market today.  Heard a chase after a raider after we had turned in; don't think they caught him.

Thursday, June 23.  Clear this morning, and very warm. Tent next to us had their meat stolen last night; a fight near the sinks, and another near the sailors' tent, early this A.M., but did not amount to much; no roll call; two more tunnels discovered, one on the north side, and the other on the south side, near us.  Brown went to the hospital good bye Brown! One man came in from the hospital today, as convalescent. He had been wounded, and *is the first one who has returned from the hospital*; they generally go the other way.  A squad of prisoners came in today, mostly from Grant's army; the 7th N.Y. Heavy Artillery seems to own most of the prisoners; they were taken at or near Petersburg; they report Petersburg as now in our possession, and that Richmond is cut off from all railroad communication with the South; that Grant has received reinforcements of 110,000 one hundred day men, and that he will not storm the city, but starve it out.  We'll see.  Drew meal at night, but nothing else; expect to draw salt and fresh beef in the morning.  Not a drop of rain today, being the second day this month.  Boys next door think one of their one chums went back on them. No wood today.

Friday, June 24.  Clear and warm this morning.  Drew salt and fresh beef about 10 A.M., the latter fly-blown; traded a ration of beef for an onion, boiled the rest, and made some soup, which we relished very highly.  Atwood sold his tobacco-box for two onions.  Took a walk on the north side; it reminds me of Chatham street, New York; it is quite as crowded, and the cries of the peddlers are incessantly heard;

"Who wants the wood?" "Come up, now, gentlemen, and give us another bet here's your chance to double your money," &c., &c. Saw a dead man carried out. Seven weeks a prisoner today. Drew meal at night, but no salt or meat. Very warm all day, and no rain. The rumor of the day is, that prisoners who had money taken from them at Richmond are to apply at the gate and receive it back. Jagers is no better, and Mulvaney and Hoffman are both sick; my diarrhea is better. A few prisoners from Sherman came in.

Saturday, June 25. A crazy man is running around naked this morning, some scoundrel having stolen his clothing. Very hot, but a good breeze stirring; clear all day. Drew bacon and salt A.M., and meal, salt and fresh beef P.M.; also a small ration of liver. Fried our liver and some beef, made a gravy thickened with corn meal, scalded our meal and made some improved cakes, and had a "bully" supper. Some 50 prisoners came in from Sherman's army. The rumor that money was to be returned to the prisoners is beginning to take a tangible form; today the sergeants of squads were furnished with blank printed rolls, with columns for name, regiment, company, number of detachment and mess; this looks like business, and has given rise to all sorts of rumors regarding paroling, &c. The work on the new stockade has been discontinued, the men having refused to work. No roll call today. Took a "bully" wash at the spring last night and tonight; the water in the creek is so coated with grease from the cook house, that it is unfit to wash with, much less for drinking.

Sunday, June 26. Drew nothing today, as the drawing

commenced on the north side. Saw a regular ring fight today, between two of the old prisoners, near the creek; they fought some fifteen minutes, when one got enough; both were somewhat scratched, but not much injured. No roll call. A party of raiders "cleaned out" Tarbell, McNeese and Nelson, of 57-1; they took boots, blankets, &c. Some few prisoners came in from Sherman, and report him near Atlanta, preparing to attack that place. The latest parole rumors are that 700 barrels of hard tack were unloaded at this depot today; that the rebs are fixing up cars to transport the sick, and that 20,000 reb prisoners are at Fortress Monroe, awaiting shipment. Fried beef for breakfast, and made beef soup for dinner; quite luxurious living for Yankee prisoners. Blackberries are selling at 60 cents a pint; wood is very scarce, as the squads do not get out half the time. Find that scalding our meal saves about one-half of it. We did not eat all our rations before, so now we will have plenty to trade off. Very hot all day. A "raider" was caught and his head shaved this morning; he sold his pint cup for $1.50, and then went at night and stole it back.

Monday, June 27. Two years ago today, I was first taken prisoner; have a mighty good sight of spending another 4th of July in captivity. A "raider" was chased early this morning, but I do not know if he was captured. Drew meal, salt and fresh beef this A.M., and made some beef tea for dinner; drew meal, salt and fresh beef P.M. A fine prospect of a general row this afternoon; the raiders were out in full force; an orderly sergeant was enticed into their tent, and robbed of $50; the raiders near the gate were contemplating an attack on this part of the camp last night; the sailors and raiders in this corner combined their forces, sent out

skirmishing parties, and made arrangements to repel the
attack, but the fight did not come off. Atwood sold a
haversack of meal, and bought an onion and a piece of
bacon, so we will live high tomorrow. A squad of prisoners
came in today; I heard that a Jerseyman of the 15th regiment
was with them, but I did not see him. Petersburg reported
taken, also Beauregard and 10,000 prisoners. Clear and hot
all day.

Tuesday, June 28. Two years ago I entered Richmond. The
night passed without disturbance. Two shots fired last night,
but don't know whether any one was hurt. A squad of
prisoners came in this P.M., among whom were some from
our regiment; [William] Ackerson, of Co. D, reports Jack
States as killed at Spottsylvania Court House, Col. Ewing as
seriously wounded, and Capt. Gaul in command of the
regiment; he says Oakley and myself are reported as taken
prisoners; Kinney, [William] Dougherty and Lovett, of Co.
D, are wounded. Drew meal P.M. A row was imminent
about 11 o'clock tonight, but did not amount to anything. A
heavy shower this afternoon, and rainy most of the night.
Very sick all night, with chill and fever, diarrhea, and
terrible pain in the right breast and side. Grant is reported
within 2½ miles of Richmond, and that he has thrown some
shells into the city; his army is said to be all on the south
side of the James river; Danville is said to be in our hands,
and McClellan, with 250,000 one hundred day men,
operating at various points. The new comers know nothing
about exchange arrangements, and we have no hope of
getting away from here before August or September; the
veterans of the 1st regiment have been incorporated with the
4th regiment.

Wednesday, June 29. Drew salt and bacon A.M. Cleared up this morning. Feel better today, but still have a violent pain in the right side. The 1st, 2d and 3d regiments started for home on the 4th of June. Drew meal and bacon P.M. About two P.M. two men came along, trying to sell a watch; Dowd asked to look at it, and did so, after which they went away; in short time they returned with reinforcements, and attacked him as he sat in his tent, with clubs, brass knuckles, &c.; he defended himself bravely, and they again departed; he came out of his tent, and put on his pants, when they again attacked him, and finally got him down, took his watch, cut out his money, (which he had sewed in the waistband of his pants,) to the amount of $170; he was badly cut up, but finally got away and reached the gate, and reported to Capt. Wurtz, who came up with him and demanded that the robbers should be given up, under penalty of no rations for one week; in a short time a guard came in, and took eight men from a tent near the dead line on our side; very soon the camp was in an uproar, for the men came into the arrangement, and the raiders were hunted from one end of the camp to the other; by dark the tumult was nearly over, but the raiders are not all caught yet; about 50 were taken outside; the issuing of rations was stopped. Heavy showers P.M. Large quantities of clothing, blankets, &c., were found in some of the raiders' tents. Capt. Wurtz deserves great credit for his prompt action in the matter, and will probably be successful in checking the operations of these thieving scoundrels.

Thursday, June 30. Very warm today. The crusade against the raiders still continues, and several were taken today; three of those who robbed Dowd are reported to be among the number; the fourth and worse one has been caught since the above writing; they are now pretty well cleared out; the sergeants of messes (90) were called up at 9 A.M. and taken to Capt. Wurtz's headquarters, where 24 of them were selected, their names taken, and 12 drawn by lot as a jury for the trial of the principal raiders; this P.M. the trial is progressing; this course is pursued to prevent retaliation on the part of our Government, to whom the whole proceedings are to be sent; it is an act of justice on the part of the Confederate authorities which the men have not expected, they supposing that no notice would be taken of their complaints; but the reverse has been the case, and we can now feel secure from the attacks of daylight assassins or midnight murderers; the issuing of rations was promptly commenced as soon as the men known as ringleaders were captured. We expect to move to the new stockade either today or tomorrow. Oak. went out as a witness; towards night news came in that Sarsfield, one of the principals, who said he "would cut Dowd's heart out and throw it in his face," had been convicted and sentenced to be hung; the trial of the others is to come off tomorrow. Drew fresh meal and meat P.M. I forgot to mention in connection with the raiders, that large amounts of money were discovered in some of the tents today, as well as watches, jewelry, and articles of all descriptions. No rain. Dowd moved his things to the outside today, where he has liberty to the extent of one mile.

# JULY

Friday, July 1. Clear and hot. Had to throw most of our meat away, it being spoiled during the night. About noon we started for the new stockade (from 49 up), and got there about 4 P.M. The raid on the raiders still continues, though in a less violent degree than on the previous occasions. Found wood very scarce in our new quarters, but lots of ants, lizards and centipedes, the latter said to be very poisonous; the boys generally do not seem to much like the change; some of the men were barely able to cross the swamp, and one man died so soon as over. A shot was fired by one of the sentries, but no one was injured. At night we drew meal and fresh beef, and made a stew. After dark, the men south of the middle stockade commenced work on it, and the sound of axes was heard during the night.

Saturday, July 2. Clear and warm. The inner stockade has almost entirely disappeared; the men south of it secured it, as they have all the axes. Drew salt A.M. Tomatoes 50cts. a piece. Drew meal, fresh beef and salt P.M. A man shot near the dead line about 12 P.M. No news. Moore (hospital steward) says the Richmond papers are blaming Lee for allowing Grant to out maneuver him during the present campaign. The supposition is that Richmond surrendered on the 1st inst. The latest parole rumor is to the effect that a captain of the 72d Ohio was here today on pass from Gen. Winder; that said Captain had been paroled, and that he told his men to keep up their spirits, for a general exchange would commence on the 7th inst. Very hot all day.

Sunday, July 3. Had a roll call today. Very hot. Drew no rations in any part of the camp. One hundred and eight prisoners from Sherman's army came in, and report him within 12 miles of Atlanta, and advancing. The man shot last night died. Baked out first hoe-cakes. The parole rumor still gains ground. Men are digging wells all over the new ground; several fights; a prayer-meeting near our tent in the evening; a bridge (double) built over the swamp and brook at the west end.

Monday, July 4. All new men taken out of the old squads and placed in new ones; the Detachments renumbered; ours is now Detachment 35, mess 1. The "Fourth" opened with a couple of fights among our men, but no demonstrations on the part of the rebels, except the wounding of a man in the hip near the dead line. Very hot, but some refreshing showers. Drew bread, salt and raw beef P.M. A raider caught stealing a blanket, was tried by one of the committees, his head shaved, and shown around camp. The carrying out of dead men is almost an hourly occurrence. Some of the raiders outside are secured in the stocks; it is reported that one of them was killed by a guard last night. Some seven or eight dead men have been carried out by 5 o'clock P.M.

Tuesday, July 5.  Roll call; another hot day.  Drew fresh beef, salt and meal P.M.  The usual parole rumors are floating around, but nothing that can be depended on.  [Clement L.] Vallandigham's (of Ohio) speech is given in one of the Macon papers of the 3d inst.; so it seems he is back in the United States.*

Wednesday, July 6.  Two months prisoners, and all tolerably well yet.  Vinegar issued today.  Very hot, but a good breeze.  A new squad of prisoners came in, some of whom are from Grant's army.  They report offensive operations suspended, and the army quiet along the James and Appomatox rivers; that sixty miles of the Danville Railroad has been destroyed, and that no communication by railroad with Richmond now exists.  Drew bacon, salt and meal P.M.  Not so hot as usual.

Thursday, July 7.  Very hot today.  Roll calls regularly now.  The day passed quiet till night, when considerable excitement was created by the passage of a large number of locomotives and cars from the direction of Americus.  The parole rumor received its quietus for the present, as there were no signs of men leaving here today.  The sick have not been allowed out for some days, there being no medicine, and most of the raiders have been sent back into the stockade.  Drew bacon, salt and meal P.M.  A class and prayer meeting at night; well attended.

Friday, July 8.  Nine weeks prisoners today.  Very hot.  About 200 prisoners came in this afternoon from Grant and Sherman, mostly cavalrymen.  Sherman reported to be shelling Atlanta.  Kilpatrick reported to have crossed the

* Congressman Clement Vallandigham, leader of the Peace Democrats or "Copperheads," was banished by Lincoln to the Confederacy in May 1863, and returned to the U.S. from Canada on June 15, 1864.

Chattahoochie river on a raid. Neither Petersburg nor Richmond taken up to the 29th of June. Washed my clothes at 4 A.M., and got them much cleaner that I expected. Rumor says there will be neither paroling or exchanging during the whole war. During the day several fights occurred, but no serious one. The prayer meeting was held at night, and promises to become an established institution of the camp. It is to be hoped so. Some members of the Christian Association (and, I believe, of the Masonic Fraternity), are the leading spirits of the arrangements. Drew salt, meal and mighty strong bacon P.M. Atwood received word that his brother is a prisoner. Extra trains of cars are still running. No medicine, and no sick allowed out, except wounded men. Several dead men carried out.

Saturday, July 9. Another hot day. A large number of prisoners (over 200) came in today from Grant's army. They report our men to have taken 55,000 prisoners; the Danville and Lynchburg Railroad destroyed, so that prisoners have to march from Petersburg to Danville; that 1200 of the 2d Corps. were cut off and captured at Petersburg, and will be here in a day or two. A heavy shower came up this afternoon, cooling the air nicely. Drew bacon, salt and meal P.M. Our stock of wood has played out, and it yet lacks six days of the two weeks in which we were to get none. Reported that some of the Third N.J. (Veterans) came in today, but I did not see any. Attended the prayer meeting at night; the interest in these meetings is increasing very fast, and several men have asked to be prayed for. The sick call this A.M. was very crowded, but the medicines are *non est.*

Sunday, July 10. Pleasant morning. Good many dead men carried out. It is said the treatment at the hospital is much better than when we first came, and that the number of deaths is materially decreased. About 6000 prisoners came in today from Grant's army, some of the 6th Corps among them; they bring no news of importance. Drew very nice bacon, meal and salt P.M. Heavy showers all around us, but no rain here. Reported that the Sixth Corps. has been reinforced and sent to North Carolina. Traded two rations of pork for a pint of beans. Preaching and prayer meeting at night.

Monday, July 11. Cloudy A.M. Atlanta reported in flames, and Johnston gone to reinforce Lee. A Charleston prisoner, captured yesterday week, told me [Maj.Gen. Robert S.] Foster had been repulsed in an attack on Fort Johnston, on James Island. A slight shower came up about 4 P.M., cooling the air considerably. About 5 o'clock P.M. a rebel guard was seen marching toward the stockade, preceded by a drum corps, playing the "Dead March," and conducting six prisoners. They entered the gate at the southeast part of the stockade, when Capt. Wurtz (commanding the camp) delivered the prisoners over to a body of the Regulators, headed by "Limber Jim." A gallows had been previously erected in the street leading from the southwest gate. The prisoners names were given as follows: "Moseby," "Murray," "Terry," "Sarsfield," "Delainy," and "Curtis."* They were all of Irish birth or extraction, except "Moseby," who was English. "Limber Jim," with his assistants, proceeded to bind the prisoners' hands, the Captain having withdrawn the guard to the outside, leaving the condemned to be disposed of by our men. When Curtis was about to be

*The men hanged were: Willie Collins, a.k.a., "Moseby"; Andrew Muir; Terry Sullivan; John Sarsfield; Patrick Delaney; Charles Curtis.

bound, he exclaimed, "This cannot be," and made a dash
through the crowd and toward the creek; he succeeded in
reaching the other side, but was arrested and brought back.
Shortly after five o'clock, the whole six were swung off, but
"Moseby's" rope broke, bringing him to the ground, but he
was soon swung up again. After having hung about fifteen
minutes they were cut down, when the crowd quietly
dispersed. So endeth the raid on Dowd, three of his
principal assailants being among those executed. And it is
to be hoped that it will also end the system of organized
robbery and ruffianism which has so long ruled this camp.

**The hanging of the Andersonville raiders.**

"Limber Jim" and his assistants were taken out of the stockade after the execution, and it is supposed they will be employed outside. A squad (1700?) of prisoners came in today from Grant's Army; they bring a report that the Exchange Commissioners have agreed on terms for exchange and parole, to commence on the 16th inst. Drew pork, salt and meal P.M. Changed our sergeant, appointing Emmett in place of Buckley.

Tuesday, July 12. Another squad of prisoners from the 2d and 6th Corps. came in today; they bring the usual amount of rumors, but nothing definite. Very pleasant day, not so hot as usual. Drew meal, bacon and salt P.M. Wood is getting very scarce. Some of the Detachments are said to have drawn rye flour. Rumored that Johnston has fallen back from Atlanta, and that "Fort Johnston," on James' Island, near Charleston, is taken.

Wednesday, July 13. Two men shot near the dead line before roll call this A.M., one was instantly killed. No prisoners came in. [Maj.Gen. David] Hunter reported to be burning bridges, railroads, &c., around Richmond. Very hot. Drew meal, rice, salt and bacon, P.M.

Thursday, July 14. Another warm day; a thunder shower last night, but did not touch us. The parole rumor revived, paroling to commence now tomorrow, but it received its quietus about noon, when the sergeants of messes were marched to the headquarters of Capt. Wurtz, and addressed by him; he stated that the Rebel Government was anxious to parole or exchange, but the Federal Government declined, because the time of so many of the men here had expired;

that he had plenty to feed us on for two years, if necessary; that he had received information that some 6,000 men inside had organized for the purpose of "tunnelling out," capturing the batteries, overpowering the guard, and releasing the whole body of prisoners; that he had sufficient force to quell any such arrangement, and if the attempt were made, he would open on the stockade with grape and canister so long as a man were left alive within it. He desired the sergeants to warn the men against entering into any such conspiracy. About two o'clock, two cannon near the southwest corner of the stockade were discharged, and great was the tumult that ensued; sergeants engaged in issuing rations, dropped their cups or knives, and fell flat to the ground, rooting their noses into mother earth like babies for their "titty"; men plunged headlong into the "dug out" tents, the brook, or any place that offered the least show, or, in fact, no show for shelter against the storm of grape and canister which they expected was soon to come hurtling over their devoted heads; cries of "lie down" and other vociferations resounded through all parts of the camp, and the writer hereof felt very much as if he would as soon be somewhere else as here, to say the very least. Nor were some of the scenes outside much less exciting or ludicrous. The rebel guards were seen "double quicking" by battalions to different points, forming lines of battle, and performing other evolutions, and in a few minutes rattling volleys of musketry at the northeast corner of the stockade, told us that they had got into position, and were ready to repel the expected assault of the "Yanks". But some of the guards who were not on the drill, took another course, for as soon as the alarm was given,    they commenced "skedaddling" for the woods, making as good time as a quarter horse. A lady walking along one of the roads, fell as if struck when the first shot was heard, and was carried by a guard into the woods, in a fainting condition. From some of the houses within sight of the stockade, the women could be seen flying for the woods, with their babies in their arms, and shawls, or whatever they could first catch up, wrapped around their heads. The tumult lasted about half an hour, when everything relapsed into the usual state of semi-confusion. Capt. Wurtz gave notice that if he noticed any unusual group of men crowded together, he would fire into them. Drew bacon, meal and salt P.M. Two shots fired by the guard after dark; don't know if any one was hurt or not. Cloudy most of the day. No sick call for several days.

Friday, July 15. Ten weeks prisoners today. Several shots fired last night and today, but have not heard of any one being hurt. It is stated that some of the men, at the instigation of the authorities here, are getting up a petition to be sent to our Government, urging an early exchange or parole. It is stated that the petition contains a threat that the signers will take the oath of allegiance to the "Corn-federacy," if their request is not complied with. The Government should punish any man who would sign such a document. Cloudy most of the day. Several tunnels discovered and filled up. Sherman's army reported to be over the Chattahootchie, and investing Atlanta. Men dying very fast inside stockades. Drew bacon, salt and meal P.M.

Saturday, July 16. Summer half gone. [Lt.Gen. Richard S.] Ewell said to have recaptured 25,000 rebel prisoners, and to be within four miles of Baltimore.* Several more tunnels discovered, one of which undermined some four yards of the

*Gen. Jubal Early, not Ewell, invaded Maryland on July 5th with about 10,000 infantry, threatening to liberate the rebel prisoners at Point Lookout.

stockade. The guards are reported to be deserting very fast. The weather for the past few days has not been so warm as at the beginning of the month. Sick were allowed out this A.M., for the first time in some days. Drew bacon, meal and salt P.M.

Sunday, July 17. A fellow who "blowed" on one of the tunnels was taken this morning, his head half shaved, and the letter "T"—for traitor—branded on his forehead, and he was then marched around the camp. It is said the reward he received from the rebels was half a plug of tobacco. We are taking a little epsom salts each morning now, to purify our blood. Atwood confiscated an axe while outside yesterday, and we have been paid some wood for the use of it. They bring in one load of wood for 10 Detachments (2,700 men). Tonight we got a better ration than usual, and gained some by renting out the axe. Drew meal, salt and five spoonfuls molasses per man at night; no meat. Two shots fired after dark; one struck a man in our street, cutting his finger, thumb, cheek and tongue; he was in the act of taking his pipe from his mouth; it was an accidental shot, the gun being discharged while in the act of capping. Some few prisoners brought in, but all old ones, nine of ten months standing, who have been kept at other places. Preaching and prayer meeting at night. A sergeant haranguing the men in favor of the before mentioned petition, which recites the treatment of prisoners, &c.

Monday, July 18. Cloudy A.M. A negro whipped outside stockade for refusing to work; he came in crying; he belongs to the sailor crowd. The men who branded the "traitor" yesterday were demanded, on the penalty of "no rations until delivered." They were finally found and taken outside the stockade, but soon returned without any apparent punishment. Rainy P.M. Reported prisoners are to be sent to Alabama tomorrow. A few prisoners came in, captured in Alabama; they report Montgomery burned, and our cavalry raiding through the State, so I don't think we will go there. Rations issued late P.M., but did not reach us. A large number of women and children are reported to have arrived here from Atlanta and Macon, fugitives from the "Northern Barbarians." Three years since battle of Blackburn's Ford.

Tuesday, July 19. Drew meal, salt and bacon A.M., and meal, salt and bacon P.M. A few prisoners came in P.M., who report that they were taken 14 miles this side of Atlanta. They report Johnston superseded by [Lt.Gen. John Bell] Hood; Montgomery, Ala., is reported burned. Men continue to die very fast, and the sick calls are very largely attended. Three Catholic priests were in attending the sick, and ministering spiritual consolation to them; they are in every day, and are the only Christian professors who visit the camp. A rebel sergeant says the Commissioners of Exchange meet tomorrow at Wilmington, N.C.; so we may look for a new lot of parole rumors in a few days. More tunnels were discovered today. A sergeant again harangued a crowd in favor of the petition, and it seems to find considerable favor with the men; it is said six men are to be sent with it. Rained a little after dark.

Wednesday, July 20. Two regiments are reported to have arrived last night; the rebels busy this morning throwing up trench works to command stockade. A tunnel was opened this A.M., about two o'clock, and men were escaping till after daylight, when the guard discovered them and gave the alarm. Negroes are busy examining wells and looking for other tunnels. A train of cars with reinforcements arrived about noon. A rebel paper states the Ewell levied a contribution on Hagerstown of $100,000, and on other placed in proportion; that he has returned to Virginia, and had a fight with [Maj.Gen. Ambrose] Burnside. The negro prisoners refused to work on the trench works, which have been built so as to command the railroad as well as the stockade. Drew meal and bacon P.M., but no salt. Considerable excitement after dark by men rushing to get out of a tunnel just opened; some 500 congregated, and the crowd defeated the whole thing, for the rebs "smelt a big mice," and double-quicked to the spot; the night was very light, and all their motions were seen. Oak. gave me a "big scare", by coming in and declaring that 2,000 men were preparing for a rush on the stockade; it made me so nervous that I did not get to sleep till after midnight. Some few prisoners came in, and report Kilpatrick within 15 miles of Andersonville. Some of the men who escaped this morning were recaptured and turned in again towards night. Cars arrived about 9 P.M., and cheering was heard outside. A prayer meeting also seemed to be in progress. The work on the entrenchments continued during the night.

Thursday, July 21. Three years since first Bull Run. The work on the entrenchments still continues, and they are assuming quite extensive proportions. A few prisoners came in from Sherman's army, captured three weeks ago. Saw Dick Wardell; he is in the huckstering business. A cavalryman cut at his throat, near our tent, but did not hurt himself much. Drew meal, salt and molasses P.M. Very warm day.

Friday, July 22. Cloudy, windy, but very little rain. Drew extra molasses A.M. and meal, salt and bacon P.M. Three men shot at the south gate by a sentry, one supposed mortally. Some four of five hundred prisoners came in, taken at various times since the 10th of May; they report a cartel of exchange agreed on, to commence as soon as the campaign is ended; Grant reported shelling Petersburg; Ewell reported returned to Virginia with loss of his artillery and baggage; the Danville railroad rebuilt. Several shots fired by sentries near the run, but no one hurt. Watermelons, $4.00; apples, 40@60c.; biscuit, 25c., corn, 30c; eggs, 35c; beans, 30c per half pint. Wood sold his memorandum book, and we had a bean dinner; At. sold his shaving brush for 10c., bet on the sweat-board and won 20 more, and Oak. sold his thimble for 30c., so we expect to have a bean dinner tomorrow. Saw Lewis Traute; he is bad with scurvy and diarrhea. Wardell gave me a biscuit with honey on it, but is was not very gay.

*Andersonville Stockade, from Capt. Wirz' Headquarters.* **After a sketch by Robert Sneden, c. 1864.**

Saturday, July 23. Cloudy and cool most of the day. Some few men came in from hospital, but no new prisoners. Drew meal, salt, rice and bacon. Parole rumors are flying thick and fast, but no reliance can be placed in them; the most prominent is to the effect that Butler has been superseded by a new Commissioner of Exchange, and that a cartel has been agreed upon, to commence August 6, five rebels for three Yankees. Confederate money went down to 20c. per $1 today, and is not much liked at any price. Saw small frying pan sold for $5. Men still dying very fast; it is agonizing to walk through the camp at night, and hear the groaning of the sick; "Mike King," Trenton sailor, belonging to the gunboat Gen. Jessup, died last night.

Sunday, July 24. Very cold last night, and suffered considerably with my feet; cloudy and cool this morning; first-rate chill and fever weather. Wardell brought me over a quarter of a water melon. We had rice and molasses for dinner, and cooked up our water melon rind with molasses, making a very good sweet-meat. Drew fresh beef and rice, but no salt. We have lived well the past few days. Men dying very fast inside, 31 carried out yesterday, and the stretchers keep going almost constantly. A big fight reported near Atlanta, and any number of parole rumors.

Monday, July 25. Another very cold night, and no tobacco. Sherman reported repulsed near Atlanta, and 7,000 prisoners and 20 pieces of cannon taken from him. [Jacob] Robinson, of 1st N.J. Cavalry, in our Detachment, died today of diarrhea. Drew rice and bacon P.M., but no salt, and the Q.M. says we must blame our own men for it. The work on the works continues, and they are making a regular dirt fort near the Captain's headquarters. Parole rumors still on the wing.

Tuesday, July 26. Slight shower P.M. Three men died within 20 feet of our tent today. A squad of prisoners arrived outside, but did not come inside. Drew rotten bacon, and threw most of it away, meal and salt P.M. Begged a piece of tobacco from Wardell.

Wednesday, July 27. One man shot while getting water, through the head, killing him instantly; he had just come in. Some four hundred or five hundred prisoners arrived, mostly 100 day men, taken in Maryland. Parole rumors are rampant. A slight shower P.M. Another man died within a few feet of our tent; most of those now dying are new recruits, enlisted last winter. Wardell let me have 50 cents worth of beans on time, and we had a bean dinner. Ambulances have been running all P.M. from depot to hospital, laden with rebels wounded at or near Atlanta. Many of their wounds had not been dressed.

Thursday, July 28. Some seven or eight hundred prisoners came in from Sherman's army, some of whom state that they were taken in the outskirts of Atlanta; a cannon shot was fired over the camp while they were marching in. The parole excitement still increases. Two shots were fired over the camp after dark. Drew meal, salt and bacon P.M. Heavy rain P.M. A man walked outside of dead line, being tired of life, but the guard would not shoot him.

Friday, July 29. A man died just in rear of our tent last night; about 30 a day inside is the average. Poles with white flags have been raised about the center of the camp, and crowds congregating west of them are to be fired on. A squad of prisoners came in P.M.; many of them from hospitals, and some were minus an arm or leg. A sentry fired at a man who pushed some wood over the dead line, and the rebel sergeant told the sentry he was a fool and never did know his business. The parole fever increases in violence, and is the chief topic of conversation. This individual is just as anxious, but not quite so sanguine, as some thousands around him. The 6th of August is now set as the time, but I will be very well pleased if we get out by the last of September. Drew meal, salt and bacon P.M. Rainy in the afternoon. Twelve weeks prisoners today. Thomas Mulvaney, of Co. B, 4th N.J.V., went to hospital, very sick.

Saturday, July 30.   Peter Smith, formerly of this Detachment, died this A.M. The parole rumor increased in fervency daily, the 6th of August being the day generally fixed on for exchanging to commence. Some of the guards now on the stockade are barely able to see over it, being 14 or 15 years old and very small. Some shots fired, but no one hurt, so far as heard from. The work on the sinks and swamp still goes slowly on. The negroes brought in a report that [Maj.Gen. Lovell H.] Rosseau was shelling Macon. Tunnels are discovered daily. Drew rice, salt and bacon P.M. Traded our meal for bread. Reported that sixty dead men were carried out yesterday, but I do not believe it.

Sunday, July 31. A Macon paper of the 29th inst. states, on N.Y. Herald authority, that terms of exchange have been agreed upon by Commissioners of Exchange, but that it has not yet learned them. This has increased the parole fever, and is the first reliable thing I have seen, so I am slightly affected myself. The rebs have induced a number of prisoners, cordwainers by trade, to go outside to work for them, and they are to go outside this A.M. The rebs are busy at work on the fortifications, and have commenced two new works, one at the northeast corner of the stockade, and the other on the northern side; they are apparently afraid of some movement on the part of our cavalry, and they keep their men in the works night and day. A number of convalescents came in from the hospitals today. Drew rice, salt and bacon P.M., but no wood, as they will not issue wood on Sundays. Atwood commenced operations with a " chuck-a-luck," or "sweat-board."

**Photograph of the southeast portion of the stockade showing the sink area. Taken by A.J. Riddle on August 16, 1864.**

*Escape from Andersonville*  **by Walton Taber.**

# AUGUST

Monday, August 1. Cloudy and misty this morning. A few more convalescents came in. Last night the work on the fortifications was continued all night, and by the flashes of lightning the rebs were seen in line of battle inside the works. They are also felling trees and forming abatis. No cars have arrived from the direction of Macon since Saturday, and it is reported that the railroad is torn up. The priest brought in a paper with the exchange item, as also did some of the rebel officers. Three trains arrived late in the afternoon from direction of Macon; ambulances were running during the day between the hospital and depot, apparently conveying sick to the depot. Drew rice, salt and bacon P.M. Rained a little P.M.

Tuesday, August 2. Some 400 prisoners (cav.) came in P.M.; they report Gen. [George] Stoneman and his body guard captured in Macon, attempting to release our officers. A large number of sick were taken out of the stockade, and either placed in hospital or taken away, we do not know which. All communication with Atlanta is reported cut off. Drew rice and bacon P.M.; wood is very scarce; half of our rice was cracked and full of stones;

traded it for bread. Heavy rain during the afternoon. The rebs still at work felling trees, &c.

Wednesday, August 3. Clear and hot, with a light shower P.M. The sick were still rushed out, some suppose to a new hospital, others think to our lines. Some four or five hundred cavalry prisoners arrived, who contradict the story of Gen. Stoneman's capture, and say it was a Col. Stoneman. Several shots fired by sentries, but have not heard of any one being hurt. Kelly and Cummings both gave us some wood, so we got along very well. Drew meal, bacon and a very large ration of salt P.M. Some 2,100 have been taken out during the last two days. Hoffman gave me one of his shirts, as mine was about "played out".

Thursday, August 4. A man shot and killed on the southern side of stockade early this A.M.; he was asleep, and got over the dead line; the guard called to him and then fired. The negroes were working all night, as we could hear their singing, which always sounds inexpressibly mournful to me, as if the wail of the oppressed was rising to heaven. Some 400 sick were taken out today, but the number inside seems as large as ever. Several shots fired P.M., but no one hurt, so far as heard from. Drew rice and bacon P.M. No roll call today.

Friday, August 5. More sick taken out, this time by Detachments, from 1 to 8, inclusive, then 35, and two others, eleven in all. About 100 new prisoners came in, from Sherman's army; they report having met the sick on the way to Macon. Drew rice and bacon and fresh beef P.M., but got euchred out of our salt and about one-half of our fresh beef. They commenced drawing in one load of wood for five Detachments, instead of for ten, as heretofore. The sick of eleven Detachments are to be taken out daily until all are out. Got a sore mouth and throat, probably from eating raw bacon. Thirteen weeks prisoners today. Two years ago we left Richmond, and marched to Aiken's Landing. No roll call.

Saturday, August 6. Two years ago today ended my first experience as a prisoner of war, and three months since my second capture. A man shot through the head and instantly killed by a sentry, at the watering place, about two P.M. Some of the cases of sickness which have been witnessed during the last few days are horrible in the extreme. One man, who lies near our tent, and who has been twice carried to the gate, debilitated with swelled feet from exposure to the sun or dropsy, chronic diarrhea, and *neglect of cleanliness*, was found to have the lower part of the body, near the rectum, eaten into holes by maggots, which literally swarmed him. He was been washed by some of the men of his Detachment, both yesterday and today, but can hardly recover, as there is no prospect of his getting in hospital for some days. By his side lies another, who is afflicted in a similar manner, and near them lies one who, although weak from diarrhea, is still able, in a measure, to help himself, but having lost all ambition, has given up hope, and desires only to be left alone to die in his filth. These sights can be seen in any part of the camp, and are not isolated cases. Drew fresh beef, meal and salt P.M. Reported that no more fresh beef will be drawn in the new stockade. Slight showers P.M. A big rumor that from 15,000 to 25,000 of us are to march to Savannah in a few days. No roll call.

Sunday, August 7. The man I spoke of yesterday as having given up all hope, died last night. He was a Heavy Artilleryman. No roll call. A detail of 13 men was made from Detachment 1 to take care of sick on the cars. A few prisoners from Sherman came in and report him shelling Atlanta, and that an exchange has been agreed on. Great excitement in camp—one of the rebel quartermasters told some of the men a general exchange had been agreed on, and some of us would go out tomorrow. Biscuit came down on the strength of the report to eight for one dollar. The worm-eaten man died this afternoon. Another sick man was brought to the same ground, so they seem bound to keep at least two sick men on the same ground. Drew fresh beef, meal and salt P.M.

Monday, August 8. No roll call. There has been no sick call nor any medicine issued to the men since they commenced taking the sick out of the stockade. It is horrible. Rainy this afternoon. Drew fresh beef, salt and meal P.M. Bringing in boards for barracks.

Tuesday, August 9. Showery all day. Another man died in front of our tent last night. There were ten dead men this A.M. on the road from our tent to the runlet. The framework of one of the barracks erected in the northwest corner of stockade. Three years today since Co. B, 4th N.J. Vols., was mustered into service. The company, I suppose, are anxiously expecting marching orders for home. Terrible rain during the afternoon, washing away the stockade in three places—two on the eastern and one on the western side, near where the run enters and passes out. The "Island" was almost overflowed. Two artillery shots were fired as signals, and the rebs manned the guns, formed line of battle, and made every preparation to resist any attempted outbreak, but the rain was sufficient to make the Yanks "lie low," without anything else. No rations issued on our side of stockade. Negroes immediately set to work repairing the breaches. A few prisoners came in from Sherman's army. They report Hood sending everything to the rear, as if meditating a retreat into South Carolina. Hope he will go soon. They also say that some prisoners have been exchanged at Fort Moultrie, and that the Trans-Mississippi prisoners are now in course of being exchanged. Rainy all night.

**Gen. John Winder (left), Capt. Henry Wirz (right).**

Wednesday, August 10. Drew one-half ration of bread and a pint of sour beans per man A.M. Drew one-half ration of bread, one-half ration of fresh beef, and pint of raw beans per man P.M. Got wood this afternoon. Rained terribly, so that we could not cook our beans. A sick call today, the first in a long time. A government wood contractor by the name of John Morris, from Herkimer county, N.Y., is buying up State money, Savings Bank checks, and other valuable securities from 50 to 60 cents per dollar. There are others engaged in the same business. Morris is a citizen, and was captured at Plymouth, N.C., and has a large amount of money with him. The wet weather for the past few days has been very hard on the sick men, and they are dying off rapidly. The work of roofing the first barrack was commenced today, and the repairing of the stockade continued.

Thursday, August 11. A dead man in rear of our tent this morning, and any number throughout the camp. Cloudy, and the air heavy and oppressive to the lungs. Some of the men on the other side having stolen the planks from the sink-head, rations were stopped on the other side. We drew bread, beef and beans. A few prisoners came in from Sherman's army, and brought the biggest parole rumor of the season. They state that they have read in the *Cincinnati Commercial* and other papers, that 550 of our officers have been exchanged, and that exchange of enlisted men will commence on the 15th inst. Atwood sold some of our buttons to the darkies for tobacco and wood. The work on the new stockade was commenced today. No sick call and no medicine. A report circulating that Fort Gaines, Mobile, has been taken by Com. [David] Farragut, also capturing

Com. [Franklin] Buchanan, and blowing up the rebel Mosquito fleet.

Friday, August 12. Bringing in boards for 2d barracks. Work on new stockade continued. Men still dying very fast. No sick call. Drew beans, a small quantity of meal, and salt and fresh beef. Lewis Traute and Cornelius Post are both very sick. The new stockade is commenced on three sides of the present enclosure. Atlanta reported evacuated (for the 77th time), and a new raid started for Macon. The roofing on the first barracks was not continued today. Some of the hospital stewards sent in for getting drunk. The 15th inst. parole rumor is spreading furiously. Fourteen weeks prisoners today.

Saturday, August 13. Hot all day. A sick call, but no one taken to the hospital. Drew beans, beef and a half ration of bread P.M. Our rations of meat have been very small for some days, one-half and one-quarter rations. A few prisoners came in, but brought us no news. A prayer meeting in the evening. Bringing in more lumber, and the new stockade is growing rapidly.

Sunday, August 14. Everything very dull and quiet. Drew fresh beef, salt and beans P.M. Thomas Mulvaney died in hospital some days ago.

Monday, August 15. A sick call this morning. Went on the island and saw Duncan; his legs and feet are much swelled, he looks thin and worn down, and looks very much depressed in spirits. [John] Rosenberger, of Co. D, 4th N.J. Vols., died today; Jos. Kline, the most profane man I ever heard, and who tented opposite to us, died today, while in transitu to the hospital. Drew bread, beef, salt and beans P.M.

Tuesday, August 16. Atlanta again taken, this time 33,000 rebel prisoners with it, and also the rebel Gen. [Joseph] Wheeler. Seven men taken out on sick call today. Great time among the Johnnies after dark; trains passing toward Macon, men yelling, guns firing, bonfires burning, and apparently a general jubilee. Slight shower after dark. The rebels are flooring and siding the run with boards, so that it will be much better than before, both for washing and getting water. Drew bread, salt, beef, bacon and beans P.M. Indiana, Illinois, Ohio and Kentucky reported seceded, and Grant in the Shenandoah Valley.

**Photograph by Riddle taken inside the North Gate as the ration wagon entered on August 16th.**

Wednesday, August 17. The regiment's original term of service expires this day, and the boys will probably start for home immediately. Our detachment commenced carrying in lumber for their barracks today. We all went out, and succeeded in getting enough firewood to last us for two weeks, so now we will commence our three meals a day again. Another sick call A.M. A notice was on the gate this A.M., cut from the *N.Y. Herald*, stating that Commissioners of Exchange had met, but giving no particulars. It was soon torn down and replaced by a written statement that the prisoners were all to be exchanged. This is supposed to be stuck up by some Yank to get the boys "on a string." Very hot. Drew bread, beef, salt and beans P.M. The nights are very pleasant. A Macon paper today pronounces Gen. [George] Thomas a bigger liar than Gen. [John] Pope. It also states that in the late naval engagement off Mobile the Yanks asked permission to bury their dead; that there are about 20,000 troops at Memphis, Tenn., operating against guerrillas, and that one hundred day regiments are constantly arriving, composed principally of *boys, invalids and negroes.* Bully for the 100 day men.

Thursday, August 18. The work on the third barrack is commenced, and the roofing of the first one has been finished. Drew bread, beef, salt and beans P.M. Pleasant day. The last *canard* of the month is now in circulation. "Grant to retire to the line of the Potomac, Sherman to hold his present position near Chattahootchie and Atlanta, the prisoners to be sent home this fall, and an armistice to obtain until negotiations can settle the war." How are you, "Mr. Armysticks!" Gold 254 in New York, according to Macon papers, so I want a new bounty. Hoffman and Atwood have something like scurvy in the mouth; hope it is not. Atwood commenced the coffee business on a borrowed capital of $00,250.

Friday, August 19. Fifteen weeks prisoners today. Showery P.M., with a heavy wind. Drew fresh beef and salt A.M., and bacon, bread and beans P.M.

**Photograph of the stockade by A.J. Riddle looking northwest.**

Saturday, August 20. Showery. Atwood increased his business by supplying two firms instead of one. Drew fresh beef in the morning, and bread, salt and beans P.M. A few prisoners came in, and report Burnside superseded, and that Grant and Lee are reinforcing Sherman and Hood. A boy died in rear of our tent, without any one knowing of it for some time. The work on the barracks continues, and the new stockade is nearly completed. Drew wood.

Sunday, August 21. Rainy all day. Rebel officers inspecting camp, among them Major Shinn, who formerly had charge of Belle Island. Drew fresh beef A.M., and bacon, bread, beans, salt and meal P.M. Letters and express boxes arrived for prisoners today, and a few prisoners came in. Three shots fired by guards at 11 P.M., but have not learned the cause. Reported that 2d and 5th Corps Army of the Potomac are now with Sherman.

Monday, August 22. Cleared up this morning. A few prisoners came in from Florida hospitals. The Macon paper states that a flag of truce boat has arrived at Charleston with important papers relative to exchange. The frame work and rafters of the third barracks are up. Drew bread, bacon, rice and molasses P.M. Stock in bank, $3, and no liabilities.

Tuesday, August 23. Clear and hot A.M. A few raiders came in, belonging to Kilpatrick, who is raiding in the vicinity of Macon. No news of importance. The Macon paper of today claims greater success for the rebel armies this summer that at any previous time, and says large forces are raiding through the North, (Maryland, Pennsylvania and Ohio,) and threatening Cincinnati. Drew fresh beef, bacon, bread, beans and salt P.M. The men are dying inside like rotten sheep. Deaths average, inside and outside, about 120 per day.

Wednesday, August 24. The sergeants in the stockade who have been commissioned but not mustered, were ordered outside this morning. Several of the sutlers went out, pretending to have commissions, but most of them soon came in again, not daring to run the risk of punishment when they entered our lines. Very hot day. Cooper cannot be found, though he may be in the camp; guess he has got out on detail or to the hospital. Drew one-quarter ration fresh beef, bacon, beans, meal and salt; also wood.

Thursday, August 25. Very hot and no roll calls. Two interesting cases were before the new Police Court today. The first, a cavalryman had been taken sick and became lousy, and was turned out of his tent by his comrades, who refused to give him his blanket, overcoat and plate. One of the officers was sent with him to the tent, and the property was handed over without further proceedings. The second case was about a sack of wheat flour, valued at $90, which the purchaser refused to pay full price for, alleging that said flour was not so good as had been represented. Saw Dick today; his oven is on "Water street," and he expects to have it in working condition by Monday next. The detachments who have hitherto drawn cooked rations are today drawing raw, and *vice versa*, so we will get cooked rations hereafter. Some thirty more commissioned men were taken out today. The work on the new stockade and on the barracks has progressed very slowly for some days. The 35th's barracks are now ready for roofing. Drew *cooked* beef, bacon, bread, rice and salt P.M., just about half cooked. A big fight on Main street during ration time. The Irishman who issues got licked; one man reported killed.*

Friday, August 26. Another hot day. A few prisoners came in, some negroes among them, who report that they came from "Prison No. 2," (Trans-Miss.,) and that all the white men there have been exchanged. This prison is said to be "No. 3", the Department of Virginia being "No. 1." The Irishman who committed the assault, yesterday, was tried today, and taken outside under rebel guard. The flour case was decided by a verdict of "no cause of action." Drew cooked beans (good ones), bacon, bread, salt and molasses P.M. Sixteen weeks prisoners today. Fort Morgan (Mobile) reported taken by our men. A man shot last night; he crossed the dead line and laid down, and refused to return when ordered by the guard, who fired twice without effect, when the infatuated Yank told him to "do his duty and get his furlough." The third ball penetrated his head.

Saturday, August 27. Two years since battle of Bull Run Bridge. Clear, and a good, cool breeze blowing. Any number of parole rumors afloat. A small quantity of United States clothing is being issued to some of the men outside. The Macon papers claim that Sherman's supplies are cut off, and that he must fight within three days or retreat and lose his reputation. Drew molasses A.M., and bacon, beef, bread, salt and cold rice P.M. Very hot all day. After dark heavy showers all around us, and some little rain here. The rebel sutler has discontinued bringing in goods, and is about to close up. The deaths are about as usual. No roll call. The Irishman who was tried for assault, was fined $20, to be

*See Appendix IV, page 194.

under guard till paid, and to be forever debarred from "holding any office of trust *or honor*" within the stockade. A cavalryman got stabbed near our tent today. Lewis Traute died today.*

Sunday, August 28. Clear and pleasant this morning. No roll call. A few prisoners came in from Sherman's corps. Men who carry out dead bodies are allowed to bring in wood on the stretchers. Today a dead man was picked up in the swamp by some men who professed to know him, his toes tied together, and preparations made to carry him out. He was laid near the bank of the creek, and in a few minutes another dead body was laid alongside of him by some other parties. The new comers claimed it as one of their regiment, and declared they had got him ready for burial, and would carry them out themselves. So they proceeded to label his breast, and the "party of the second part" tore off the label, whereupon the "party of the first part" pitched into them, and a regular "muss" took place over the two corpses. Both parties have been reported to the police. Drew beans and bacon A.M., and bread, beef and salt P.M. Post is very sick. The prisoners report hard fighting near Atlanta. The latest parole "chin" is to the effect that the Commissioners have agreed to exchange man for man, according to rank, and are now waiting for the terms to be ratified by the two governments. Free negroes are to be exchanged, but slave soldiers returned to their masters. War "chin"—that Grant has cut communication between Lee and Beauregard; also, that Sherman has been compelled to fall back from Atlanta on account of short rations.

---

*Sgt. Lewis Traute, age 30, of Co. I, 2nd N.J. Cavalry was captured near New Albany, MS., on February 25, 1864.

Monday, August 29. Two years since second Bull Run. Morning clear and pleasant. Atwood opened a sutler "shebang". A fight took place this morning between two sick men about a piece of corn bread; as neither one was able to rise on their feet, they did not hurt each other much. A small squad of prisoners came in from Sherman's lines, who confirm the report that he is falling back towards Chattanooga. Some terrible cases were carried out to the doctors, but brought in again. Parole "chin"—that our government refuses to ratify the terms agreed on by the commissioners. Drew beans, bacon, beef, bread and salt.

Tuesday, August 30. Clear and hot. Capt. Wurtz is not dead, as has been reported, but has been ill, and is now recovering. Two of the barracks are roofed, and the framework of two others erected. Wood is very sick, and Bellerjeau is afflicted with diarrhea; Atwood has sore gums and rheumatism, and I feel a little sore at nights. Deaths still average over 100 per day. Grant reported falling back. Drew fresh beef, bacon, beans, bread and salt (cooked rations), also raw rice.

Wednesday, August 31. Cloudy and cool. Some few prisoners from Sherman came in. War "chin"—that Sherman fell back on the left, drawing Hood after him, then threw in his right wing, and captured 22,000. *Humph.* Parole "chin"—that the Governments have agreed to the terms arranged by the Commissioners. The rebs are placing two outside lines of stockade around the original enclosure, and about fifty feet from it; the two outside lines are, apparently, about sixteen feet apart, and are to be filled in with sand, making a formidable entrenchment, in addition to the forts already erected. Drew beef, bread, beans, bacon and salt P.M. Last day of summer.

*The Cells of Andersonville* by **Walton Taber, 1890.**

# SEPTEMBER

Thursday, September 1. First day of autumn, and an exciting one. Rebel papers in camp stating that exchange arrangements are all completed. John Wood, of Co. D, 97th New York, (conscript,) has been messing with us for some time, and for several days has been very ill with some disease of the breast, attended with diarrhea and loss of appetite; calling me to him this morning, he gave me his pocket-book, containing the pictures of his wife and child, (a little girl,) three receipts from Adams & Co., (express,) acknowledging money sent by him at different times, six letter stamps, and a few private memoranda; he also gave me his knife, silver pencil case and gold pen, and two pipe reeds; his post office address is "Williamson, Wayne county, N.Y., near the P.O.," and his wife's name is Mary Ann Wood. If he does not recover, and I am released, I shall forward the things to her; his orders were to take care of them until he got better. No roll call. Wood died about nine o'clock in the evening; before his death he gave me a piece of soap, some needles, thread, and some other trifling articles; he died very easy. Drew bread, rice and beef P.M.

Friday, September 2. The slave negroes are being separated from the free ones. After roll call, Atwood, Getty, Lamphy and myself started to carry Wood out; we got to the gate, and found thirteen bodies in advance of us; the heat of the sun was too much for Getty and myself, and we came back; the others went out and brought in a considerable quantity of wood, Atwood bringing a large limb of a tree. The number of deaths in the stockade averages over thirty per day. Capt. Wurtz is on duty again. Parole rumors of all kinds are in circulation. Drew fresh beef, bread, beans and salt. Seventeen weeks prisoners today.

Saturday, September 3. Cloudy. A number of convalescents came in from the hospital; the sick and wounded are being brought from Macon and other places; no medicine for several days. The rebel papers state that President Lincoln has flatly refused their offers of exchange, probably on account of the clause remitting recaptured slaves to their masters. I honor the man for his integrity, but cannot help a feeling of regret, and almost dismay, at the prospect of the coming winter. But "let the right prevail though the heavens fall." I shall do my best to keep alive. The work of roofing our barracks commenced today, and was about half completed. The papers state that Hood has been circumvented by Sherman, who has gained Hood's rear, and is now on the Macon and Atlanta railroad, some 25 miles from Macon; that Hood must leave Atlanta to its fate, or have his army totally annihilated. Quite a change from their tone of a few days since. So I suppose all our hopes must now rest on the success of Sherman. Drew fresh beef, beans, bread, salt, P.M.

Sunday, September 4. Cloudy, and a little rain A.M. More convalescents came in from the hospital. Some of the boys tunneled out last night, and several shots were fired at them, but no one hurt. Report today states that [Maj.Gen. William] Rosecrans has reinforced Sherman with 30,000 men; East Macon was reported on fire this morning. Hoffman has the scurvy in the mouth, and rheumatism in the hip badly, and Oak. is weak with the diarrhea; my health is better today than for a few days past. Clear and hot P.M. Drew bread, bacon and beans A.M. Deaths continue to average 120 per diem. The two outer lines of stockade are nearly completed. Drew fresh beef and salt P.M.

Monday, September 5. Clear and hot. A man sleeping in his tent was shot by a sentry and instantly killed last night, whether accidentally or not I could not learn. Hoffman's mouth is getting very bad, and Oakley is no better. The roofing of our barracks is completed. Glorious news today from Sherman; the Macon papers state that Hood is the worst whipped man in the Confederate States; that he was not whipped only out of Atlanta, but 27 miles beyond it; that [Lt.Gen. William] Hardee is cut off from Hood and two corps belting at him, while six corps are pitching into Hood; that Hood blew up his stores and abandoned his heavy guns, and that Sherman had taken 15,000 prisoners. HOORAY! in big letters. A transport has arrived at Charleston with rebel prisoners, and Yanks were sent in return. Drew bread, salt, rice and molasses. The rations are growing very small, not enough for two meals per day. A few prisoners came in. Cornelius Post, of Co. D, 4th N.J. Vols., died today of scurvy and starvation. He expressed his willingness to go, and his confidence in a happy hereafter. His mouth has been in such a state that he has been unable to eat the rations for some days.

Tuesday, September 6. Four months prisoners today. Drew boiled rice, salt and beef P.M. Great excitement in camp. Orders for the first 18 detachments to be ready to move at a moment's notice. The men are cheering, locomotives whistling, and the camp is wild with excitement. The point of destination is said to be Charleston. Lewis Traute died last Saturday week.

Wednesday, September 7. The hospital men are moving to the cars. Ten detachments went out of the stockade, but five were compelled to return for want of transportation. One of the rumors in regard to this movement is, that our government has refused to exchange, but informed the rebel authorities that if they would parole the prisoners held by them, they (the U.S.) would recognize the parole, and feed both parties; prisoners, in preference to refighting the rebel prisoners. *Humph!* We moved our quarters into the barracks this morning, and find them much pleasanter in the daytime. I have heard that Cooper is located in the northeast corner of the stockade, but so far have been unable to find him. All day long squads were going out, and towards night orders were given to various detachments to hold themselves in readiness to move. During the afternoon the sick were left behind, and it is rumored that the men will have to march some twelve miles. The idea prevails very extensively that it is a "skedaddle." The sick being left behind gives color to the rumor. Drew bread, beef and cooked beans. Very hot today.

Thursday, September 8. Detachments have been going out since one o'clock A.M. the story the rebels circulate is, that our government has sent able-bodied men, and demands the same kind in exchange. The camp begins to look thinned out in some parts, but not in our end. The practice of "flanking" is being practiced very extensively; also, the selling of chances. About noon we were ordered to leave the barracks and take up our old ground, as the barracks were wanted for the use of the sick, who are now being left behind. Awtood, Bellerjeau and myself moved out, leaving Hoffman behind, as he is hardly able to walk, and took up our old camp ground. Oak. and myself are together, Atwood stopping down at his "shebang." Mat. Hill and his party are going to try to "flank out" tonight. Drew beans, beef, salt and half a pint of meal, per man, today; no bread.

Friday, September 9. Eighteen weeks prisoners today. A great many sick men were taken to the hospital; Alfred Hoffman, of Co. B, 4th N.J. Vols., was among them. Report states that the rebs have met with a severe defeat near Richmond in attacking Grant's works. Mat. Hill and his party did not get out last night, but are still waiting. Hardee is reported killed at Lovejoy Creek, this side of Jonesboro. The lower camp begins to show the effect of the thinning out process. The sutling business is about "played out." The surgeons were today inspecting the sick in the barracks. Richmond is tonight reported evacuated, and Lee trying to form a junction with Hood. Drew bread, beef, rice and salt. The old part of the stockade looks almost like a deserted camp.

Saturday, September 10. Some 800 left here at 3 A.M. The dead and living pass out together, for the stretchers are going from sunrise to sundown. We expect our turn in a day or two. A great many sick men have been left, and suffered terribly. Some cases have been found of men not having anything to eat for three days. The rebels are doing all in their power to alleviate the miseries of these unfortunates, and have ordered our internal police to seek out all such cases and have them conveyed to the barracks. Over 400 extra rations were issued to the sick (inside) yesterday. Atwood took his things tonight with the intention of "flanking out." Robbing the sick in the barracks is extensively practiced. A large number of them were today conveyed to the hospitals, and one or two trains sent from hospital to exchange. Drew bread, rice and molasses. The Richmond "chin" still prevails.

Sunday, September 11. Trains still running. The last detachment left the south side of the brook this A.M. It is contemplated running four trains per day, about 3,000 men. Clear and pleasant this morning. Detachments, from 22 to 33, received orders this afternoon, and marched over the creek. Atwood got off last night. A shot was fired after dark, but I have not heard that any one was hurt. Some of the rebels who say they have been down with the train, tell us our men give each of the new arrivals a piece of soap and a towel, and start them for the water, making them throw away all clothing and come back naked, when they are furnished with new suits. A rebel sergeant says the cheering was terrific when our men first caught sight of the transports. The sick in the barracks are dying very fast. Drew meal, rice and beef P.M. Some of the men still think we are going to another "bull pen."

Monday, September 12. The detachments ordered yesterday are not all gone (at 8 A.M.). The trains have not started. We expect orders some time today. Cooper came to see me today. He is in 58-2, and looks very well. One of the exchange "chins" is that two months' prisoners get 30 days furlough; 4 months', 50 days; six month's and over, with less than one year to serve, a discharge! Oh, my! Drew bread, salt, rice and molasses. We received orders about seven P.M., and started immediately. Flankers nearly crowded us out, but we succeeded in getting through. Rations were issued at the depot, a quarter of a sheet of bread, and about a pound of bacon to two men, to last two days. Oakley and myself are together. We arrived at Macon about eleven P.M., and laid there till nearly daylight, when we started on the Georgia Central Railroad towards Augusta.

Tuesday, September 13. Arrived at Augusta about six P.M. Suffered considerably for water. Ate all our bacon, but have bread enough for tomorrow. Traded a gold pen and extension case for tobacco, for want of which we have been suffering for some days. Changed cars after dark, and started towards Columbia. Traveled slowly all night.

Wednesday, September 14. Two years since South Mountain. Very little sleep last night; the cars are much smaller than those we started in; all sorts of rumors in circulation—no exchange—another "bull pen," &c.; we are all abroad as to our destination or ultimate disposal. Arrived at the junction below Columbia about 3 P.M. and changed cars, taking the road towards Charleston; traveled all night, arriving at Florence Junction (?) (65) about 3 A.M. on

Thursday, September 15. After being kept on the cars until about noon, we were marched into a field, and formed in divisions, suffering greatly for want of water; rumors increasing in number and size—no exchange—new "bull pens," &c. We, most of us at least, feel much disappointed at not seeing more signs of an exchange; the current story among the rebels here is that there is to be no exchange. Some of the men (5,000) are reported to have been sent to Columbia, others to Charleston and other places; one party was sent back from Charleston today, and joined us this afternoon; there are only about 3,000 men here, and over 15,000 must have left Andersonville; negroes in large numbers have been set to work this afternoon, and it is supposed they are making a "bull pen" for us. Several men escaped on the way up, and the indications are that a heavy stampede will take place tonight; the scurvy has affected Oakley's and my own legs so much that we can scarcely walk, or we would probably be among the number. The men made a rush on a rail fence this afternoon, in spite, of the efforts of the guards to prevent them. Rations commenced coming towards midnight, by the single wagon load, and continued coming in slowly all night; about a sanitary cup of meal, and less than a quarter of a pound of bread was issued—a very small ration, without meal or salt.

Friday, September 16. Nineteen weeks prisoners today. Last night was very cold, and we suffered considerably; we have but one blanket, having left our other one behind us. The chronic diarrhea has taken hold of Oakley again. About sundown the whole camp was fell in line, and counted off in Detachments of 300, and messes of 100. After dark the men commenced running the guard, singly and in squads of all sizes; there was a "pop, pop, popping," all around us, and there would have been but few men left in camp by midnight, if the rebels had not commenced the issue of rations, which they did about 8 P.M.; we received each a pint of corn meal and a small piece of corn bread, without salt, and later yet bacon was issued, about a quarter pound per man. Jagers arrived here today, and is bunking with us. A considerable number of men are supposed to have escaped during the night. One dead man was carried out today, and several are lying in a critical condition.

Saturday, September 17. Roll call this morning. Very cold again last night. A rush was made by the boys this morning, past the guards and on to a rail fence, which soon disappeared before the onset of the Yankee depredators; some of the men broke through the woods, and soon the "pop, pop" of musketry was heard from the picket line beyond; but few, if any, succeeded in escaping. A rebel quartermaster rode by this morning, and told the boys we had come on them by surprise at first, but hereafter we should have plenty of rations, such as sweet potatoes, rice, flour, salt, meal, &c. Oh, my! We'll see. The rebels say they do not expect any more prisoners to arrive here. All hopes of an exchange are at an end for the present, and we must possess our souls with what patience we can. I like this place better than Andersonville for many reasons, but water for drinking is scarce, and or washing there is none; but a few days may effect an improvement in this respect; it is a consummation devoutly to be wished, for, from my *color*, I am somewhat in doubt as to whether I am a mulatto or a quadroon—I certainly don't look like a white man. But, hurrah for the flag! It is currently reported that some of our men have taken the oath of allegiance to the Confederacy, and been sent to Castle Thunder, Richmond, to be held as Yankee deserters. They ought to be sent to the D—ry Tortugas. We are dreading the equinoctial storm very much. The people here will not take greenbacks, as a general thing. Corn, $1 per ear (scrip), sweet potatoes, 50 cents a piece, &c. Watches command exorbitant prices, $10 silver watches bringing from $60 to $80. Yesterday I traded a pocket-book for 12 ears of corn, equivalent to $12; the book was probably worth 50 cts. at home. During the afternoon farmers came in with carriages and on horseback, bringing back skedaddlers; most of the latter had their bosoms stuffed full of grub, vegetables, &c., and one had been furnished with a clean shirt and drawers by some charitable secesher. Drew rice and salt P.M. It is reported (but very doubtful) that 12 or 14 skedaddlers were killed by the pickets.

Sunday, September 18. Cloudy, with sprinkles of rain. Drew beans and bacon A.M. Oak. traded the looking-glass for a lot of sweet potatoes. Farmers still bringing in skedaddlers. The men are let out in squads of 100, with only four guards, for water. Some 500 sick arrived from Andersonville. Got a bad cold on breast. The sick were taken outside of the guards and kept by themselves. Showery P.M. Sick taken out of camp.

Monday, September 19. Cloudy again. No news. Drew beans, bacon, rice and salt, A.M. All the sick who could walk ordered back into camp.

Tuesday, September 20. Cloudy and drizzles of rain. Our rations are very short. The planters hereabouts use but little wheat, rye or corn for bread, substituting rice, which is a staple of the country. We get about six tablespoonfuls of rice, and a pint of beans, one-third, at least, are worm-eaten and rotten, and are thrown away, so that our allowance comes short. Drew beans, rice, bacon and salt. Water very scarce; only 50 allowed out at a time.

Wednesday, September 21.    Cloudy and rainy, the equinoctial, I suppose. Saw a planter pass, on horseback, 15 hounds with him, "*hunting Yankees, I reckon.*" Exchange rumors beginning to revive; Sherman and Hood to exchange 2,000 prisoners (special), commissioners meeting near Charleston semi-occasionally, &c. Drew bacon, beans, rice, wheat flour and salt—a good ration. Traded a pocket-comb for bread and tobacco. Rained hard after dark. A man wounded close to our tent just after dark, by a sentry.

Thursday, September 22. There are five pieces of artillery now commanding the camp. The guard who shot the prisoner last night says he thought he saw a man crawling up to him on his hands and knees; the ball went through the wrist and entered the side, not dangerous. Cleared up this morning. Wells are being dug by various detachments, but we have no facilities for washing clothes, and are getting very dirty. Several of the guards and the major express the opinion that we will not be here long. Major Brown, in command of the camp, has lately been a prisoner himself, only being exchanged some five or six weeks since; he seems to do all in his power for our comfort, as do the guards, with the exception of some boys of from 14 to 16 years of age, who assume more airs than a major general. Drew bacon, beans, meal, flour, rice and salt, in mighty small quantities. Heavy showers during the day.

Friday, September 23. Twenty weeks prisoners today, got the scurvy, got a good ducking, got very little to eat; *contra,* got good spirits, got hopes of getting out, and ain't half so bad off as many around me. Rained terribly this morning, putting out our fires and overflowing our tents completely, with a promise of more to come. How are you, equinoctial? Let 'er rip! Rained very hard throughout the day, by spells, but cleared up towards evening. Drew about four tablespoonfuls of meal, three of rice, and a teaspoonful of salt, but no meat or flour. Five butchers were taken out of camp this afternoon, so we expect to get fresh beef. A rainbow, so hope the storm is over.

Saturday, September 24. A man was shot near our tent and died a few minutes after; he was quite an old man, got over the dead line, was ordered back by the sentry, a boy of some 14 years, and finally killed. Clear and warm this morning. Drawing fresh beef; drew about a quarter pound for yesterday; this P.M. we drew about a quarter pound of fresh beef, half pint of meal, about four spoonfuls of rice, and a little salt; no beans. "Small by degrees," &c. I begin to think that even Mark Tapley, Esq., would have conceded some credit to a man for being "jolly," under all the circumstances of our position. Heavy showers. Some of the detachment sergeants are getting up another "petition," this time to the Confederate Government, for a parole. Ugh! Talk of a break-out before the stockade is finished; it will end in talk; the work on the stockade goes on steadily.

Sunday, September 25. Very cold last night, but the sun shines brightly and warm this morning (8 A.M.). This individual has seen some pretty hard times before being "grafted into the armee," and he will just stand the Southern Confederacy one pretty tight hitch this winter before "caving in." When they bring me down to an allowance of one scanty meal per day for weeks in succession, terminating the course with three days on raw turnips and half-ripe persimmons, I shall begin to think of "the days of yore," and acknowledge the corn that they have got me in a tight place. Till then, "like patience on a monument," &c.—we drop the subject. (6. P.M.) Since writing the above, we have drawn about three-quarters of a pound of fresh beef, to last for two days, but no salt, meal, rice or beans; so I reckon the Confederacy is about "trying it on." (9 P.M.) Waked up by a terrible shout of "rations." Turned out and received some five spoonfuls of meal and a modicum of salt, which we immediately manufactured into "stir-about," devoured, and turned in again. Hooray for the Cornfed.! Cold as blazes; a number of sick were sent in this morning, all who were able to crawl. A rumor that the ten detachments are to leave here tomorrow; hope so.

Monday, September 26. One of the guards came in with his pockets full of grub, which he gave to some of the sick. Two men died last night from cold and exposure. Clear and warm this morning. Before roll call we drew a sanitary cup of rice to each two men; after roll call we drew three-fourths sanitary cup of meal, three spoonfuls beans, and teaspoonful salt. Confederacy stock went up on sight, but not half so high as I hope it will go before the fall campaign is over. Jagers, Oak. and myself are the only 4th Reg't Jerseymen I can find in this crowd. The rest are at Columbia, Charleston, Savannah, and other places. Afraid my book won't last till the end of my imprisonment. No signs of a move.

Tuesday, September 27. Clear and warm this morning, and not so cold last night as the two preceding ones. Some of the men took French leave last night, and were fired at, but not hurt. Saw Lamphiere this morning; he has been in the hospital, and looks very thin. Two more Jersey 4th men are here; [Patrick] Curran, of Co. C, [Augustus] Pitman, of Co. I, and some others whose names I do not know. Drew beans, beef, meal and salt. A regiment and eight pieces of artillery left this camp for the front today. Major Brown commands the camp.

Wednesday, September 28. Drew three spoonfuls of beans, four of meal. Sick today; pains in loins, legs and head, bilious. The men, rendered desperate by starvation, commenced running out this afternoon, and for an hour there was an almost incessant popping along the line. Two men were wounded, one in the hand, and one in the hip. Threats made of a general rush; a new piece of artillery brought up. Showers P.M. A large number of sick taken out.

Thursday, September 29. Feel quite well this morning. A small cup of meal issued to each man just at daylight. After roll call, molasses was issued, five spoonfuls per man; also, five spoonfuls of rice, one-half of a small sweet potato, and salt. Officers are in here today taking names of men who will take the oath of allegiance to the Cornfed. government, or some such oath. Quite a large number put down their names. Three men were shot last night, one through the bowels. Considerable excitement over the allegiance affair, but a large majority of the men stand firm by the flag.

Friday, September 30. No sleep last night. Drew one-half pound of beef this A.M.; nearly a small cup of meal, one-half cup of rice, one-half cup of beans, and teaspoonful of salt. Some of the men are backing down from taking the oath, as spoken of yesterday, saying they misunderstood its import. Very probable. Davis is reported to have made a speech at Macon last week, stating that one-half of the Richmond army is now absent without leave; that he must have his well men for the front, and his sick and wounded home; that thousands of Yankees have died at Andersonville of home sickness, and that, for the sake of humanity, he must accede to "Beast" Butler's terms, and exchange a negro for a white man; if the *original nigger* could not be found, then a substitute must be provided. Very pleasant, saith the Frenchman, but "stop a little." Also, that the Georgia people must not be discouraged, for in a short time Sherman's army would be scattered to the four winds of heaven, by a more disastrous defeat than Napoleon's at Moscow. The ball goes on. Some fellow kited out after dark, and a sentry fired at him, the ball going about as high as a two story house. Wonder if it didn't hit some secesh picket. A few sick men taken out. Saw one dead man. Twenty-one weeks prisoners today.

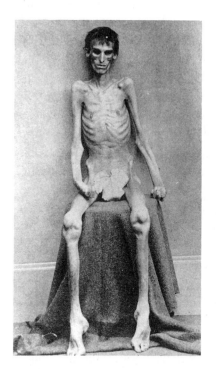 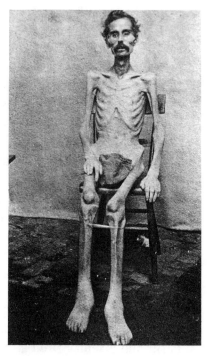

**Two survivors of Confederate prisons.**

# OCTOBER

Saturday, October 1. Warm last night, and slept well. Feel better this A.M. A slight shower at daylight. Drew one-half hard tack, two spoonfuls of meal and some salt per man, and about four pounds of beef for 250 men. We lost our beef, some other crowd getting it. We ate our rations at one meal, and got up hungry.

Sunday, October 2. (Sundown) Some 1500 Yankees arrived this A.M. and were marched to the stockade, where we soon followed them. The camp is a very rough one. No rations issued yet, and our sufferings from hunger are terrible. God help us, for man seems to have forsaken us. Light in the head, awful pains in the legs, and scarcely able to stand alone. (9 P.M.) They have just finished issuing rations, having commenced about an hour after sundown. Drew large rations; large sanitary cup of meal, one-half a cup of hominy, one and a half spoonful of flour, four of molasses, and a teaspoonful of salt. A larger ration than we have drawn for weeks, and we needed it. The Major says we will get more rations at twelve o'clock tomorrow. The stockade is some 400 yards square, with a run of water through it, the bottom of which is covered with a black mud, so that it will hardly be fit to wash in. New detachments were organized; we are now 16-2, 4th mess.

Monday, October 3. A dead man was found in the brush near the run this A.M. We have had two good meals from our rations, and have some left yet. Cloudy and misty, and very warm; showers throughout the day. The men are taking the oath of allegiance very fast; I have heard that some 640 were left behind in camp who had taken it, and that some 300 have signed today. Hunger is driving many of these men, while others intend to desert at the first opportunity; others again, dare not venture to re-enter our own lines, on account of their repeated flagrant violations of military law (straggling, &c.); and some few act without properly understanding the pledges required of them. All the afternoon bags of flour and shoulders of beef were kept in sight of, but not issued to, the hungry crowd within the stockade, thus giving fresh vigor to the allegiance movement. After sundown rations were issued: one sack of flour to 300 men, two sacks of beans to 900 men, two quarters of beef to 300 men, and about four quarts of salt per 100 men.

Tuesday, October 4. Clear and warm this morning. Some few dead men lying around camp. A large number of the working squad were sent in this morning, having declined taking the oath of allegiance. It is now reported that some 540 have taken the oath and are to be dispersed throughout the rebel army and navy. Sold their birthright for a mess of pottage. Drew a small sanitary cup of rice, three quarters small sanitary cup of flour, seven spoonfuls of molasses, and a little salt. The Major says we can write home, and send for clothing and provisions, which will be delivered to us. Stop a little!

Wednesday, October 5. A man was killed on the dead line at the water place, this morning about sunrise; Oak. and Jagers are trying their luck fishing for catfish, or "bull prouts," as most of the men call them. There was nearly an occultation of a star with the moon last night, and the superstitious are certain that the war is about over. Some 1,500 prisoners arrived from Charleston; they report that the rebel papers say that Richmond is nearly taken, and are advocating submission to Gen. Butler's terms in regard to exchange. Hope they do. Drew three-fourths small cup of meal, small cup of beans, quarter pound meat, and salt.

Thursday, October 6. Five months prisoners today. Formed into detachments of 1,000, and placed in regular streets; our detachment changed to 11-2; we are now in the S.W. corner of the stockade. Jagers found Foster, and got his blanket; it came in good season, for a violent storm arose at dark, drenching us to the skin. The creek here is covered on the bottom and sides with a thick black mud, so that it is impossible to wash anything decently. Drew a small sanitary cup of beans, half cup of meal, and a little salt. [Lt.Gen. Jubal] Early reported defeated in the valley, and Lee reported defeated near Richmond, with heavy loss. Hope so. Rained most of the night.

Friday, October 7. Twenty-two weeks prisoners today. Cloudy and dull. Drew eight spoonfuls molasses about noon, and a small sanitary cup of flour near dark; no meat, meal, salt; "things is workin'." Some more prisoners arrived from Charleston. Some sucker stole our wood knife.

Saturday, October 8. Very cold last night and this morning. Drew a small sanitary cup of rice, same of flour, half do. of meal, teaspoonful salt, four tablespoonfuls molasses, one-third cup of beans, a splendid ration, and one that set the whole camp at work cooking. It is said a Colonel from Charleston is now in command of this camp, who formerly had command of the Charleston prisoners; the latter all speak well of him, and say he is a good man for rations. Atwood came to see me. I have been unwell for several days with rheumatism.

Sunday, October 9. Clear and very cold. Drew a large sanitary cup and one-quarter of flour, small sanitary cup of meal, and a good ration of salt, this morning. Pains all over me, and symptoms of cold on the bowels. Some prisoners came in from Charleston, including all the sick. Mat. Hill came in, and stopped to see me; he says Farragut's fleet is at the city, and hot work is expected there. Some heathen stole our little sanitary cup.

Monday, October 10. Warm and pleasant this A.M.; my health, and consequently my *courage*, much improved. The Israelites of old were punished for longing for the flesh-pots of Egypt; if I should be punished for longing for the flesh-pots of Washington st., Trenton, N.J., fearful would be my fate, for they are before my mind's eye continually. Oh, for a huge slice of corned beef, cabbage, turnips, potatoes, with a good, nice, *motherly* loaf of bread before me, and topped off with about four plates of "bag pudding," with or without "huckleberries." Hush, child, hush! A man was shot through the leg at the water place, this morning. A band of musicians playing outside at daylight. Trains running all night; from the repeated cheering, we judge troops are going from Charleston to Richmond to participate in the grand struggle; I wish I was there, but I suppose all is for the best. Fremont is reported to have withdrawn in favor of Lincoln; glory to Fremont.* The Charleston papers say McClellan stands no chance; glad to hear it; "war to the knife, and knife to the hilt" against any compromises with the accursed institution of slavery. (See how brave I get under a hot sun.) 480 men are reported to have taken the oath today; most of them are men who had no blankets or shelter of any kind, others took it intending to escape. Drew meal, flour and salt, same as yesterday. The boys "raided" on such of the "oath" men as had anything, taking every thing, even their tin cups.

Tuesday, October 11. Warm and pleasant this morning, and not so cold last night as during the two previous ones. Oak. and myself had quite a row last night, and indulged in mutual recriminations to a considerable extent, but all is "calm as a summer's morning" today. The rebel officers are reported to have said that we would not be here long, that Davis has accepted Butler's terms, &c.; but I have given up all faith in such stories, and am contemplating the erection (or rather excavation) of a mud domicile for my winter quarters. More men sent out on the "oath." Drew a large sanitary cup of flour, two and a half spoonfuls of meal and four of beans; no salt, meat or molasses. The men are now being formed into Detachments of 1000.

Wednesday, October 12. Warm and pleasant. Reported that sailors and marines are to be exchanged. Deaths outside reported to average about 30 or 35 per day. There are

*John C. Fremont withdrew from the election on Sept. 17th.

supposed to be about ten or twelve thousand men here. No roll call, as sergeants are busy forming the men into thousands. Drew small sanitary cup of flour, four spoonfuls beans; no salt, meat or molasses yet. Clothing from the Sanitary Commission is being issued to the sick. Several thousand negroes are at work on the outside of the stockade, banking up, building platform for artillery, &c. A sick call at 2 P.M. Roll call hereafter is to be at 6 A.M.; so we will have to "root out" earlier.

Thursday, October 13. A slight shower last night, doing no harm; cooler today, but not unpleasant. Drew a small sanitary cup of hominy, half do. of flour and meal, (mixed) eight spoonfuls molasses, teaspoonful salt. We are evidently on half rations, or less, again; for two days they have three sacks of flour and one of meal to 300 men; now they give only five sacks of breadstuffs to 1000 men. Wonder how long this rotten old Confederacy will be able to hold out. I suppose they will try to breathe till Abraham Lincoln is re-elected, and then die, and leave no sign except some 25,000 half-starved Yankees, and a hetacomb of slaughtered husbands, sons and fathers. Well, roll on, Father Time, and bring the day of deliverance quickly, for my bones ache at the thoughts of this winter, and the blue water runs from the corners of my mouth, when I think of the "stews" of our army's winter quarters. Ate our rations at one meal.

Friday, October 14. Commenced our mud house. A large number of men going out to take the oath, starved and frozen out; the men raided them, taking even their shoes and stockings. The nights are bitterly cold, and we suffer much. After 1 P.M., and no signs of anything to eat yet. God help us. Our knees tremble, black spots are floating before our eyes, and our heads are dizzy with weakness; but our hearts are still strong for the flag of the Union, and the rights of the poor white man. After sundown rations were issued, one-half small sanitary cup of beans, half do. hominy, one do. of meal; no salt or meat till tomorrow; but we did not have to go to bed with craving stomachs. The negroes today were singing a song I had not heard them sing before: "Your head is rotten, and you don't know nothin'; and the yaller gals say you don't know. *Chorus*—You don't know nothin', and you don't know; you're a great big nigger, and you don't know nothin'." They sing this for hours, keeping time with their bodies and pounders. One good white laborer would do more work in a day than ten of them, the way they work here; they commence work at sunrise, take from one hour and a half to two hours for dinner, and stop at sundown; they seem happy enough, but-------. A piece of artillery is now mounted on the S.W. corner of the stockade, only about 12 yards from our tent; something that look like earthworms are visible about a quarter mile from the S.E. corner. 28 weeks prisoners today.

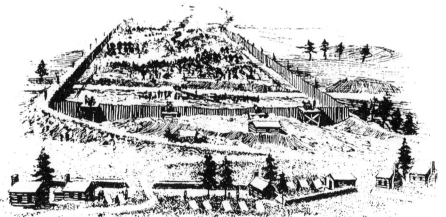

*Prisoner of War Camp, Florence, South Carolina.*
**After a sketch by Robert Sneden, 1864.**

Saturday, October 15.  Fresh beef was issued to the sick today.  About four spoons hominy, small sanitary cup fine meal, one do. beans, eight spoonfuls molasses, teaspoonful salt, and no rations to be issued to the camp tomorrow. More men went out to take the oath; they were guarded today, to prevent the men raiding on them.  We threw sand to roof our tent, and it broke down once, but we fixed her up again.  Terrible pains in back and legs, and hardly able to walk.  Boiled some of our beans, with meal dumplings, and sweetened them with molasses, a new dish, but anything for variety.

Sunday, October 16.  The lieutenant of the guard came in this A.M., and ordered a "raid" on the sutlers in the main street leading from the gate, which was promptly carried out.  The idea prevails, and is probably correct, that the sutling business tends to keep us on short rations, as it gives the rebs a splendid chance to line their own pockets.  All the money in the camp is in the hands of a comparatively small number of men, who are speculating on the necessities of the remainder.  It is reported that hereafter no meal, flour or salt will be allowed to be sold by sutlers.  Our own men outside, who deal out rations for the camp, are suspected of stealing from our allowance to supply sutlers, and share in the profits.  About 5 P.M. some of the men at the gate told the Colonel [J.F. Iverson] in command, with tears in their eyes, that they were suffering from hunger.  He immediately ordered an issue of rations, and we received about four spoonfuls of beans, do. of hominy, small cup of meal, teaspoonful of salt.  He says as long as there is food, the men shall have it.

Monday, October 17. Tore down our tent again, and fixed up a blanket over it. The sergeant of the 1st 1000 is on trial for stealing and selling rations. More men out on the oath. No rations at all issued today, except to the police; the Colonel said he had not the rations, but they were coming tonight, and he would issue them by moonrise, all of which he did not do, of course. He exchanged greenbacks with some of the men, dollar for dollar, saying that Confederate money was as good outside as our own, and forbade the reb sutlers from taking anything but Confederate money; he also confiscated some bread, and divided it among the sick. Cloudy tonight, with every prospect of a storm.

Tuesday, October 18. Small patters of rain today. Drew small cup of meal and two spoonfuls flour, just after roll call, with a promise of more after a while. Our names were taken for blankets this morning, but I doubt our ever getting them, though rumor says there are 10,000 outside for us. We hear no news, and there is a great scarcity of rumors even. About 11 A.M. we received quarter pound fresh beef, large sanitary cup of beans, small cup of rice, spoonful of salt, being more by one-half than we have received any day lately. Very cold at nights, and firewood very scarce. Suffer much with my legs.

Wednesday, October 19. Clear and warm today. No men have went out on the oath for some two or three days. Drew small cup and a half of flour, same of meal, two spoonfuls beans, spoonful salt, six spoonfuls of molasses, (five bags flour, five meal, one hominy, one beans, per 1,000 men). Rumor says Sherman has whipped Hood again, Gen. [Joseph] Hooker bringing his company up "on end," as usual, the fighting "end ways." The police today took the large woodpiles, and divided it.

Thursday, October 20. I find that I will have to encroach on pages originally intended for other matter, in order to record the loaves, fishes and corn meal doled out to us in this land of darkies and the shadow of death. I sincerely hope that before this new supply of stationery gives out, I may have to record our transportation to the land of three meals per day and cold victuals left—to the land where potatoes are *not* $10 per bushel, nor a penny hot roll sold for 25cts. postal currency—to the land where every bean does not have three bugs and a worm, and where a louse born this morning does not became a great-grandfather by noon, with a posterity of 250 alive and kick—no—biting. Speaking of lice, we kill from 50 to 200 per day each, most of them very large, and have come to the conclusion that the sand must breed them; we find them in our hair, whiskers and every where. Drew small cup flour, same of meal, three spoonfuls beans, one spoonful salt, six of molasses. Blankets given out—four to 100 men—no show for us.

Friday, October 21. Warm and clear this A.M. Drew small cup meal, one-half cup flour, half cup beans, no salt or molasses. Reported that Lee has been defeated near Richmond, with a loss of 22,000 men; that Pennsylvania has gone Republican at the State election on Tuesday. The 1st 1000 was moved over the creek, to make room for the hospital, which is to be brought inside. 24 weeks prisoners today. Drew one and a half square inches brown soap.

Saturday, October 22. Clear but cold; a north-west wind, cutting like ice. Drew six spoonfuls molasses, teaspoonful of salt, (yesterday's back rations, the rebs say,) then drew half small cup beans, small cup hominy, half small cup meal. We do make two meals out of these rations, but they do not overload our stomachs, nor is there much danger of our getting the gout. Sergeant [John] Foster, of Company K, went out on the oath on Monday; poor fellow; the rebs took his shoes when they captured him, and he was very poorly clad, as in fact we all are.* They are issuing small lots of clothing, one article generally to those most in need. Very cold all day, and a promise of an awful night. Several hundreds through the camp lost their rations by breaking rank, men being absent, &c. Pennsylvania today is reported to have gone Democratic. The hospital moved inside stockade.

Sunday, October 23. One man from each 100 taken out to chop wood. Slept better last night than for a week past, notwithstanding our fears of the cold. Warm this A.M. Drew small cup and a half of meal, half do. of beans, spoonful salt, six spoonfuls molasses.

Monday, October 24. Getting ready to send for a box after election; a rather risky business, but I don't see how I am to avoid it. They are still issuing clothing in small dribs. Rumors of some kind of an exchange, but no faith in it. Drew small cup of meal, one-half cup hominy, four spoonfuls beans, five spoonfuls rice, eight spoonfuls of molasses. Saw Mat. Hill, and he gave me enough tobacco to last me a week, and my legs pain me dreadfully. The typhoid fever is spreading extensively throughout the camp.

*German born, Twenty-six year old Sgt. John Foster swore the oath to the Confederacy and survived to return north in April 1865. Foster never filed for a pension and it is unsure what became of him after the war.--Service record.

Great excitement just about sundown, occasioned by a paper coming into camp stating the evacuation of Richmond, and that a special exchange of 20,000 is to take place immediately, the rebels to retain the negro prisoners against the surplus we hold.  Main street was in a *furor*, men dancing, cheering, jumping, shouting and singing, as if Bedlam were let loose, and the inditer of these lines turned in and didn't sleep a wink till after midnight, on account of thinking of ham, eggs, pies, puddings and—lice.  Oh, that the news may be true!  The officers say they will commence taking men out of here on Thursday next.  Amen!  Jagers drew a shirt today; Oak. and self got nothing.

Tuesday, October 25.  Clear and cold.  Bad show for breakfast, on account of wood, but Nicholas Lamb, 2d U.S. Infantry, gave me a good piece of maple, and several of fat pine, for which may the Lord bless him.  Big breakfast; corn dodgers, rice coffee, with a red pepper in it, and roasted beans.  The camp is calmer this A.M., but every one is talking exchange.  Hope I won't want any box.  Nicholas brought me a small paper of baking soda today.  Some of the boys are worried with fears that we are to be sent back to Camp Sumter; hope not.  The artillery around the stockade was taken away today, and the artillery camp at the northeast corner has disappeared.  Drew small cup and two spoonfuls of meal, two spoonfuls hominy, small cup of beans, six spoonfuls of molasses, and one spoonful of salt.  Very cold at night now.

Wednesday, October 26.  Cool A.M., but a warm day. Negroes fixing stockade, which has tumbled in at the swamp.  Reported that Sherman has whipped Hood again.

The Colonel talks of roofing sheds in the stockade, to be finished by January. Drew small cup and two spoonfuls of meal, small cup of beans, and six spoonfuls of molasses. Reported that 10,000 are to be exchanged, all from Savannah, so we are out in the cold again. "Let er' rip." Last report says Sherman is awfully whipped, and driven clear back to Missionary Ridge. Hurrah! Go in, Lemons!

Thursday, October 27. Cloudy, but warm. No wood to cook with, and no men allowed out to get any. Slight sprinkles of rain through the day. The exchange rumor still prevails. Drew small cup of some dark looking substance; some of the boys said it was rye flour, some one thing, and some another; anyhow, we made dumplings and a cake of it, and it tasted very well. Drew also small cup of beans, usual quantity of molasses, and a spoonful of salt. Nicholas Lamb brought me two nice pieces of wood about dark, and a nice piece of tobacco. This man has been very kind to me during our short acquaintance, and I will not soon forget him. Showery till about 11 P.M., when it cleared up. We spent about as comfortable a night as usual, but Oak. had a chill, and has the chronic diarrhea pretty badly.

Friday, October 28. Clear and cold this morning. The men are losing faith in the exchange reports, and are again becoming depressed in spirits. The bad weather has a great influence on us, as we feel encouraged or depressed as the weather is pleasant or boisterous. The oath excitement has all died away, and if any men are taken out now, it is done in a very quiet manner. Twenty-five weeks prisoners today. Drew small cup of flour, small cup of beans, usual quantity of molasses.

Saturday, October 29. Warm and clear this morning, but cold last night. Duncan's son lies near the swamp, very low; [Daniel C.] Cole, of our regiment, looks very bad, Curtin and [Charles H. Freas] Freese, of Co. K, are both bad with scurvy.* Hugh Williams gave us a yam last night, and we boiled it in our soup this morning, making it much better than usual. It is the first I have ever eaten, and seems to be a cross between a turnip and a sweet potato. Our 100 lost their rations by seven being missing, for whom our sergeant could give no account. Big thing—and we see it very plainly this *saving* one hundred rations to the Confederacy, because a sergeant cannot account for men, or because some men miss a roll call, cut the rations from a hundred. Go the length of your rope, old Cornfed. Sold a plate for 30 cents, bought 25 cents' worth of what they call sweet potatoes, and five cents' worth of red peppers, chopped them up fine, and borrowed two spoonfuls of corn meal, made a potato soup, ate it, and bade defiance to starvation and the Cornfed. for another twenty-four hours. Hurrah for the Union! I've got another plate left to sell yet. The reb. papers say there is a fleet of war ships and transports off Charleston and Savannah, but they do not know whether they mean mischief, or are bringing prisoners. Nicholas brought me over half a pot of beans, so we did not go to bed hungry. The camp drew fresh beef.

Sunday, October 30. Our 100 has a new sergeant. This A.M. is cold, cloudy and disagreeable for empty stomachs. Beginning to think of selling my inkstand, and letting the memorandum slide. Hard times, wait a little longer. Just

*Twenty-two year old Charles H. Freas was paroled at Savannah, GA., on Nov. 30, 1864 and arrived in Trenton, N.J., on Jan. 26, 1865. He married Jeanette Lynn in 1871 and had four children. He died in 1918.

after roll call, Nicholas came around again, bringing me enough meal to make a nice hoecake, and told me to come to his tent. I went, and he gave me a piece of beef, a mess of beans, some flour and some salt, and we had as good, if not a better breakfast than if we had drawn our regular rations. The sun came out warm and bright, and everything looks pleasant. Hard times, come again no more. Some sucker stole our little plate this morning, so we have no plate at all now. So we go. Drew small cup and a half of coarse meal, 4 spoons of beans, 6 of molasses, and a little salt. The meal is something on the Camp Sumpter order, but not quite so bad. Oak is helping Mat. Hill to build a chimney today.* The exchange rumors are increasing in number, but there seems to be no foundation for them, except that large numbers of rebels are in the camp daily, trading for watches, rings, shirts, or anything they can. Talk of the Yankees being a trading people—these folks beat them all hollow.

Monday, October 31. Warm and pleasant, but cloudy most of the day. Drew 1½ small cup of meal, same of hominy, and usual amount of molasses. The Colonel says the camp must be cleaned and kept clean, or he will discharge all the policemen, and all the sergt's of 100 and 1000. The dead carried out daily number from 30 to 50—mostly chronic diarrhea, or cold on the bowels. Many of the sick have no shelter of any kind. Details were made today to bring in brush, and an attempt is to be made to get things in rather better order.

*Mathew Hill was born in Miford, Pa., in 1838. He enlisted in Co. G, 9th N.J. Infantry on Feb. 15, 1864, was captured at Drewry's Bluff, Va., on May 16th., and was sent to Andersonville on May 23rd. Hill was paroled on Nov. 30th and arrived at Camp Parole, Md., on Dec. 5, 1864.--Service record.

# NOVEMBER

Tuesday, November 1.  A cold, cloudy, windy, and very disagreeable day.  The attempt to police the camp is still going on.  Cleared up warm after noon.  Drew 1½ small cups of meal, 1 small cup of beans, and received a promise of fresh beef and salt "after a while, if it comes." It did come—to the gate, but not inside, and will be made to count on tomorrows rations, thus keeping us out of a moiety of our already small allowance.  This game is very often played of late, and seems like a contemptible way of doing Yankees out of grub.  Perhaps if I was on the *other* side of the stockade, I could see it in a different light.

Wednesday, November 2.  Woke up in a cold N.E. rain storm.  Jagers and Oak. raised some wood; I begged some tobacco from Mat. and traded a ration of fresh meat (in prospectus) for a yam, and we made a "bully" kettle of soup.  Good weather for the oath—they were taking coopers and shoemakers out on it yesterday.  Drew one half large san. cup of meal, ¼ lb. of beef, and tablespoon of salt; molasses to be issued "if it comes." It did not come.

Thursday, November 3. Stormy yet—a terrible night. Begged some wood from Nicholas, and made a pot of mush, which warmed us up a little. Both Oak and Jagers sick. Rained by spells all day and night. Drew double rations of molasses, small cup of beans, and same of meal—so they *did* pay the back ration of molasses. About 9 P.M. we took down one of our blankets and wrung the water out, covered ourselves up and shivered until

Friday, November 4. About 3 or 4 A.M. the wind changed to the N.W. and the weather became colder by some degrees. Jagers raised a stick of wood, and we got some breakfast. The day was cold and wintry, but the Haymaker was around.* The deaths have increased in number during the past few days (during the storm). 26 weeks prisoners today. Drew small cup of meal, same of beans, salt and molasses. Very cold all day.

Saturday, November 5. Clear, but windy, and very cold. A large number of men went out to take the oath—frozen out. Horrible! Horrible! The bad weather tells fearfully on the sick—they are dying off very fast. Over 1000 are supposed to have taken the oath today—many of them in the last stages of chronic diarrhea. I cannot find it in my heart to blame these men, but, God helping me, I will lay my bones in this accursed soil, rather than ever assume a semblance of respect or allegiance to this hell-born conspiracy against one of the best, if not the very best, earthly governments there ever existed. God bless it. The Welshmen's two chums went out, and he is bunking in with

*A nickname for the Sun.

us tonight.   He is a hardy fellow—and has been in the country less than one year, but has more pluck than many "to the manor born."

Sunday, November 6.   A regular Indian summer day. Descriptive lists were given to the sergt's of hundreds this morning, to be filled up with the name, birth-place, and when and where captured, of prisoners.   A number of men who were drunk last night were taken out for punishment(?) this A.M.   Rumored that 10,000 sick, wounded, and convalescents are to be exchanged shortly.   A man shot and killed near the dead line about 4 A.M.   Reported that the Reb. took $2,000 in greenbacks from one of the men they took out today, *for punishment.*   Some few men went out on the oath.   We drew half a small cup of flour, 1½ of beans, molasses and salt.   Six months prisoners today.

Monday, November 7.   Drew cup and a half of meal, cup of beans, and usual molasses.   No wood has been issued to the camp since Saturday week, and we have hard work to even half cooked rations.   Considerable excitement in regard to the coming election.   The Rebel Congress is said to meet today. The U.S. and the C.S. to exchange cotton, blankets, &c. Oh, my eye!

Tuesday, November 8.   The polls opened in the stockade about 9 A.M., and were kept open about two hours.   The vote was about 100 for McClellan to 900 Lincoln.   The 7th 1000 polled over 700 Lincoln, to 86 McClellan.   It was a regular election scene and a regular election day—wet and disagreeable.   Drew meal, beans and molasses.   Lost our wood by our detail shysting.   The nights are very warm.

Wednesday, November 9. A man shot (accidentally, I believe) in the hospital this A.M. Warm and pleasant. Confed. scrip has been selling for some days at $10 for $1 in greenbacks. Cole, of Co. I, 4th N.J.V., died this P.M, from exposure and privation. Drew meal, beans, molasses, and wood. No news, except that the Charleston papers say there has been no arrival of sick or wounded prisoners, but that the flag of truce boats meet tomorrow. My feet are very sore around the toes—probably rheumatism.

Thursday, November 10. A warm but drizzling, misty day. It was poor Nicholas Lamb who was shot in the hospital on Wednesday last. He belongs to the 2d regiment U.S. Infantry, and has been the best friend I have met in prison, though an utter stranger to me. I am glad to learn that he is not seriously wounded; the ball struck him near the cap of the knee. Drew meal, beans, salt and molasses. We have lived very well for some days, by Davis bringing down peppers, yams and potatoes, which the sutlers give him for carrying water, &c. The papers today state that medicines, &c., have been ordered to Savannah, for the use of the rebel prisoners expected to arrive there.

Friday, November 11. Cloudy and cold. All the sutlers but one closed up by the rebs. A few cooking utensils distributed. Drew rice, flour and molasses. Came across Tom Heward, of the *True Democrat*, and had a long talk with him.* Reported that Kentucky gives McClellan 40,000

*Sgt. Thomas Heward, Co. H 10th N.J. Inf. was captured at Cold Harbor on June 2nd; and sent to Andersonville. After being paroled in February, he was placed on a train at Wilmington. A fellow prisoner later testified, "Heward must have fell from train in his sorry state (the train being very much crowded) and was killed along the road at some place." Heward left a wife and three children.--Pension File.

majority, and New York city 45,000. Well, guess he will want it all, and more too. 27 weeks prisoners today.

Saturday, November 12. Warm and pleasant. Gangrene cases taken outside, where a new hospital has been erected. Drew meal, beans, salt, and our 1,000 got a barrel of salt beef instead of molasses, supposed by a mistake, as only two Detachments got beef; it was a happy mistake. The bridge over the swamp is nearly completed.

Sunday, November 13. Clear and warm, but a cold wind. Drew fresh beef, (and a good ration of it, too,) salt, meal and rice. No news as to election yet, but the rebels concede Uncle Abraham's election for another four years. Some 75 dead bodies are said to have been carried out today. Clothing is said to have arrived outside for us. Loud cheering outside tonight.

Monday, November 14. Reported that exchange commences *tomorrow.* "Tomorrow—'tis the thief of time." Said that fifty-odd bales of blankets have arrived outside for us. Hope so. Last night was bitterly cold, and ice formed in quite large quantities down in the swamp. Towards night a number of new prisoners came in, sailors, &c., captured within 40 miles of New York harbor. Drew meal and molasses. The papers of the 12th state that exchange arrangements have been perfected, and will be carried out immediately, with all the rapidity possible; hope so, but my faith is weak. The nights are bitterly cold, and we suffer much, but the days are warm and pleasant. There is said to be a full suit of clothing outside for every man here. Rumors of all kinds in regard to exchange are afloat. Davis' message is said to recommend the employment of negroes as pioneers, engineer corps, &c., a sort of yielding the point on the negro question.

Tuesday, November 15. A squad of prisoners came in from Columbia; they report all the prisoners, except officers, sent away from there. Clothing is being issued to the working squads. Drew meal, hominy, salt and molasses. Saw Wardell today, and he gave me some tobacco, which "saved my life" for 24 hours at least.

Wednesday, November 16. Clear and hot. Some few of the Columbia prisoners went out on the oath; there were several deserters among them. Drew fresh beef, flour, meal and salt.

Thursday, November 17. A man shot at but not injured. Some three or four hundred "galvanized Yanks," clad in rebel uniforms, were turned into stockade during the morning; they had taken the oath, and done duty in the rebel service, and give various reasons for their being re-transferred. The general opinion is that an exchange is about being effected, and that the rebels prefer having their own men back. Went over and saw Wardell, who made me stay to dinner, which was quite a treat, and astonished my bowels considerably. The day was very hot. Drew small rations of meal, rice and salt, but a very fair ration of beef.

Friday, November 18. Cloudy but warm. The 5th Georgia Infantry, which has been guarding us, left for Macon this morning. The rebel papers state that it is supposed Sherman has started from Atlanta on his winter campaign through the

Cotton States. Drew rice, salt and molasses. A tunnel was discovered today. 28 weeks prisoners today.

Saturday, November 19. Rainy. No rations to be issued until all shovels are turned over at the gate. Drew yellow meal, salt and fresh beef; so the shovels must have been turned in. Drew wood, for the first time in three days. Rained all night.

Sunday, November 20. Rainy and cold. Sherman reported at Macon, and Kilpatrick at Milledgeville. Exchange rumors rampant. Drew large ration of flour, and small ones of salt and beef. Terrible night.

Monday, Misery—horrible—steady rain since before daylight—starvation—cold, and tent full of mud and water and lice. Terrible! Another tunnel discovered, and more suspected to exist. No rations till all are discovered. Drew nothing but wood. Severely cold at night.

Tuesday, November 22. Very cold and cloudy. No rations. Sold the frying pan for $1.25, and bought potatoes, which eased us a little. Terribly cold at night. Drew wood.

Wednesday, November 23. Some men froze to death last night. A tunnel discovered, but said not the right one. Drew large rations of rice, meal and salt. Terrible suffering throughout the camp; many men with their feet frost-bitten, &c.; Jagers' feet are frozen. Reported that Gen. Stoneman has been appointed agent of Commissioner of Exchange; that special exchanges are all stopped; that a general exchange commences tomorrow. Hope so, but don't believe it.

Thursday, November 24. This is said to be a National Thanksgiving day in the United States; I feel thankful to Almighty God that my life has been spared so long, and that my condition is so much better than that of thousands around me, and pray fervently that I may be spared to see my friends at home once more. Roll call at noon. The day warm and pleasant. A man escaped last night by climbing the roof of the reb sutler's shanty; the guard fired at him, but did not hit him, and they put the hounds on his track, but he made good his escape. Drew small cup and a half of meal, and a little salt.

Friday, November 25. All hands marched to the other side, and counted on their return; the other side *vice versa*. Sherman reported playing the deuce with the railroad communications, &c. Drew small cup and a half of rice; no salt, or anything else. 29 weeks prisoners today.

Saturday, November 26. Drew sanitary cup of meal, and a little salt. Reported that they are paroling the sick; short rations anyhow. Weather like Indian Summer, except that the nights are very cold.

Sunday, November 27. Clear and warm. Exchange and war stories very plenty, but no papers in camp for several days. The sick sent away, and the worst cases selected from the 1st 1,000, (veterans excepted, it is said). Drew meal, flour and bran, ate it at one meal, and went to bed hungry last night.

Monday, November 28. Three shots fired by sentries last night, said to be at a crazy man wandering over the dead line; "dead as a nit." Part of the 3d 1,000 went out today. The men are beginning to fear another "bull pen". Drew large cup of meal and a good ration of salt.

Tuesday, November 29.    The 3d 1,000 still going out. Trying to trade my inkstand for tobacco. Did trade it for a ten cent piece of tobacco. The 3d 1,000, after being partly taken out, were sent back; all kinds of stories afloat in consequence. Sherman cutting the railroad, capturing a train, &c. The rebs. say more men will be sent on Thursday. Drew large sanitary cup and a half of flour. Clear and warm. More prisoners come in from other prisons.

Wednesday, November 30. Clear and warm. First sick call for several days. Drew one half sanitary cup of meal and same of new beans, with a little salt.

# DECEMBER

Thursday, December 1. First day of winter, and very warm. Roll call over the creek. Drew sanitary cup of meal and a little salt. Lice terrible. All kinds of rumors, but nothing reliable, about Sherman.

Friday, December 2. Thirty weeks prisoners today. A regular Indian Summer day. Drew sanitary cup and a half of flour and a little salt.

Saturday, December 3. Drew one and a half sanitary cup meal and a little salt. Reported that Gen. Winder is coming here to take charge, with Capt. Wurtz as Commissionary of Subsistence. The 2d and 3d 1,000, which left for Savannah some days ago, returned, and report railroad communication between Savannah and Charleston cut by [Maj.Gen. Robert] "Foster's niggers." Report that exchange is agreed upon under the old cartel, parole every ten days and exchange every three months. Hope so.

Sunday, December 4. Roll call over the creek. Drew one and a half small cupful of rice and a good ration of salt. Buried one of our blankets to try to kill the lice.

Monday, December 5.  The 2d 1,000 is being re-examined; only the paroled men were taken out.  Rumor says exchange is played out again.  Drew sanitary cup of meal.

Tuesday, December 6.  Seven months prisoners today.  Gen. Winder visited the camp.  Drew sanitary cup of meal, salt, and six spoonfuls molasses.  The 3d 1,000 has orders to be in line at 7 A.M. tomorrow.

Wednesday, December 7.  3d, 4th, 5th and 6th 1,000 examined and sent out.  Oak. and Jagers went, leaving Davis and myself. *  Drew rice and sweet potatoes.

Thursday, December 8.  All the 1,000 were finished today. Drew meal, sweet potatoes and salt.

Friday, December 9.  The 1st, 2d and 3d were re-examined today; some more men taken from them.  Very cold, the coldest day we have had.  Davis got off, leaving me without a tent mate; moved in with Emmett & Co.  Drew meal, salt and sweet potatoes.  31 weeks prisoners today.

Saturday, December 10.  Roll call this A.M.  Rainy and cold.  We all suffer with sore eyes.  The men who were picked out yesterday are still outside, waiting for transportation.  Drew meal, beans and salt.

Sunday, December 11.  Roll call over the creek.  Heavy thunder storm last night, and bitterly cold today.  Some new prisoners came in from Sherman and from other prisons. Drew wood.  Drew rice and salt.

*Twenty-three year old William H. Jagers was exchanged  and returned to Trenton on January 25, 1865.  Thirty-six year old Samuel Oakley Bellerjeau was mustered out on July 9, 1865.  No pension file exists on either soldier.

Monday, December 12. Warmer this morning. Drew wood, rice and salt. Made and ate three quarts of boiled rice for supper, and could have eaten three pounds of bread and sausage on top of it. Very cold all night.

Tuesday, December 13. The working squads all went out to work today. Drew meal and salt. At about 11 P.M. seven trains came from direction of Charleston, apparently laden with troops. It is supposed one regiment left here, as they marched by with martial music. The rebs celebrated the anniversary of Fredericksburg by firing guns, &c.

Wednesday, December 14. Cloudy. The 1,000s were again examined, and some 800 men taken out; none from Emmett's tent. Drew meal and salt.

Thursday, December 15. Clear and warm. Roll call over the creek. Drew wood, salt and meal. Reported that 1,500 of the men who left this camp have been drowned.

Friday, December 16. Some 400 prisoners came in from Salisbury. Drew meal and beans. Very warm. 32 weeks prisoners today.

Saturday, December 17. Warm. Exchange rumors are at a discount, and the men are in the dumps. "No more exchange till the end of the war." Drew meal, beans and salt.

Sunday, December 18. Number of negro prisoners arrived from Foster's army and other points; also a number of galvanized Yanks. The latter last night robbed the former of their money, clothes, kettles, &c., and the darkies are recapturing them; several fights in consequence, the nigs invariably victorious; they have the most friends, as the boys are generally down on the galvanized individuals; some of the darks have been prisoners 17 months; they were told they were sent here for exchange. Firing commenced at Charleston on Friday last. Drew meal, beans and salt.

Monday, December 19. Drew meal and salt. Rumored that the nigs are recognized, and that a general exchange commences at Wilmington on Thursday.

Tuesday, December 20. Some 1,000 galvanized Yanks from Charleston were turned into the bull pen this A.M.; they talk about general exchange. Rainy and gloomy. Drew meal, salt and beans. Rained all night. Reported that stockade is building at Columbia.

Wednesday, December 21. Rainy; our tent almost filled with water. Drew beans, salt and meal, the best ration for a long time.

Thursday, December 22. Cleared up last night very cold. Drew meal, salt and a very small ration of sweet potatoes. Some more Yanks came in A.M., Hughes and Ladd with them; Ladd is to stop with us; he gave us all some tobacco, which "done us proud".

Friday, December 23. Clear and cool. Drew meal and salt. Ladd bought a bushel of sweet potatoes, ($13,) and we ate them boiled and roasted, going to bed for once with a full belly. A number of galvanized Yanks came in.

Saturday, December 24. Clear. Drew meal, salt and sweet potatoes.

Sunday, December 25. Christmas Day. An extra roll call across the creek. A report has been circulated that the Colonel had promised a ration of meat today, but we did not get it, rather a smaller quantity of meal, potatoes and salt being issued. Ladd bought two quarts of beans and a pint of salt, ($5.00). Rained very hard from dark until after midnight.

Monday, December 26. Cloudy. Drew meal, salt and potatoes.

Tuesday, December 27. Cloudy. Drew meal, salt and sweet potatoes. Heard thunder or cannon during the night.

Wednesday, December 28. Rainy A.M. Reports of surrender of Wilmington, N.C.; fighting at Georgetown, &c. Drew meal, sweet potatoes and beans.

Thursday, December 29. Very cold. Drew beans and molasses.

Friday, December 30. Very cold. Thirty-four weeks prisoners. Drew meal, salt and sweet potatoes.

Saturday, December 31. Windy and blustery. Drew meal and salt. Rainy A.M.

# JANUARY

Sunday, January 1, 1865. Very cold; roll call across the creek. New working squads organized. Drew meal, salt and molasses. Blankets terribly lousy.

Monday, January 2. Not quite so cold, but too cold for comfort. Wood rations very small. Drew meal and salt.

Tuesday, January 3. Clear and cold. Detailed to police the street, thus earning the first extra ration I have ever made in the Confederacy. Drew meal, salt and molasses. Rainy P.M.

Wednesday, January 4. A man shot by a sentry for speaking to him. No working squads out, and all paroled men sent in. The wood in camp collected and divided. Clear but cool. Drew meal, beans and salt. No wood brought in. Most of the paroled men (shoemakers, &c.,) from Florence sent in; they have been cutting "shines."

Thursday, January 5. No wood yet. Drew meal, beans and salt. New working squads paroled.

Friday, January 6. Eight months (35 weeks) prisoners. Rainy, but cleared up P.M. very cold. The butchers all sent in. Rumors of a general exchange. Drew meal, beans, sweet potatoes, and salt.

Saturday, January 7. Very cold, high wind. Drew salt, meal and molasses. Paynter traded his 2 quart measure for tobacco.

Sunday, January 8. Ordered across the creek, but the order countermanded. Drew meal, salt and molasses. Some sailor prisoners came in. The guards have received orders to shoot any man who addresses them. Clear and cold. Exchange talk prevalent.

Monday, January 9. Clear and warm. Drew meal and molasses, no salt. The names and descriptions of the 1st and 2d 1000 being taken.

Tuesday, January 10. Rainy and blustering. Drew meal, salt and sweet potatoes. Another armistice reported.

Wednesday, January 11. Clear and pleasant. Drew meal, salt and sweet potatoes. Descriptive lists of our 1000 taken.

Thursday, January 12. Went and saw Wardell; he gave me a quantity of siftings, and we made an extra cake and pot of gruel, which came very acceptable. Drew meal, salt and sweet potatoes.

Friday, January 13. Some forty men taken out for the oath. Drew meal, salt and beans. Pleasant weather. 36 weeks prisoners.

Saturday, January 14. Cloudy and cold A.M., but clear P.M. A few more men (foreigners,) went out on the oath. Drew meal, salt and molasses.

Sunday, January 15. Clear and warm. Roll call across the creek. Wardell gave me a huge plate of beans and dumplings, which astonished my "innards" considerably. Drew meal, salt and molasses. A man shot and killed by a sentinel for addressing him.

Monday, January 16. Cloudy and cool. A few more men out on the oath. Drew meal, salt and molasses. Exchange chins beginning to obtain; 20,000 to be exchanged by the 16th of February.

Tuesday, January 17. Clear and cold, with high winds. No men out today. Drew meal, salt and molasses; Wardell gave me some siftings, so I had an extra corn dodger.

Wednesday, January 18. Drew meal, salt and molasses. Clear and warm, a regular spring day.

Thursday, January 19. Clear A.M.; cloudy P.M. Saw W. H. Edmonds' brother; he was blown into Charleston harbor while on picket. Drew meal, beans and salt.

Friday, January 20. Cloudy and misty. 37 weeks prisoners. Drew ¾ pint meal, ¾ pint beans, ½ table spoonful of salt. Commenced raining at dusk, and rained steadily all night.

Saturday, January 21. A wet, misty day. Drew nearly a quart of meal, and half a pint of beans, with a little salt.

Sunday, January 22. Scurvy breaking out in my mouth, and skin generally disordered. Frightened! Paynter and Getman are both sick with a kind of fever. Drew meal, salt and beans. Cloudy and showery all day and night.

Monday, January 23. Cloudy all day, and rainy at night. Paynter and Getman both pretty sick. Parole talk pretty abundant, but none worth noticing. Drew meal, salt and beans. Edwards came to see me.

Tuesday, January 24. Clear and cold. A few men went out to take the oath. Drew meal, salt and beans.

Wednesday, January 25. Clear and cold. Emmett sick; three sick in the tent now. Drew meal, salt and beans. Laddie taken sick P.M.; all down now but myself.

Thursday, January 26. Clear and cold. Serg't Gordon says the Colonel states that there is an armistice of sixty days. A special sick call tomorrow for the 3d or 4th time. Drew meal, beans and salt.

Friday, January 27. Clear and cold. The special sick call countermanded after we had got the sick men out of the tent. Drew meal, salt and beans. Very cold.

Saturday, January 28. Very cold. Took Paynter up, but could not get him into hospital. Not well; cramps in stomach, and pain in breast. Drew meal, salt and beans, best ration in a long time. Edmonds brought us a stick of wood. Traded meal for beef—our first meat since November 20.

Sunday, January 29. Clear and more pleasant. Roll call across the creek. A few prisoners came in, sailors and soldiers. Drew meal, salt and beans. Wardell is working outside.*

Monday, January 30. All very sick—almost helpless.

Tuesday, January 31. All very sick. Drew meal, beans, salt and molasses. Rations growing smaller.

# FEBRUARY

Wednesday, February, 1. Clear and warm. No improvement in our condition—terrible coughs and cramps in the bowels, verging on to chronic diarrhea and inflammation of the bowels. Drew meal, beans and salt.

Thursday, February 2. No better. Drew meal, salt and beans.

Friday, February 3. No better. Same rations.

Saturday, February 4. No better. Same rations.

Sunday, February 5. No better. Same rations.

*Sgt. Richard Wardell was paroled at N.E. Bridge, N.C., on March 1st; reported to Camp Parole, MD., March 12th, and arrived in Trenton, N.J., on May 25, 1865. Wardell was killed in 1911 by an automobile in New York.

[Tuesday, February 7th, Mr. Forbes succumbed to the systematic starvation and bad treatment of the rebels, with his dying breath blessing his country. The Diary was brought to Trenton by Peter J. Edmonds, of the gun boat Sonoma, (see Diary Jan. 19, 1865,) who was with him when he died.]*

After the war, Warren Lee Goss, a survivor of Florence Prison wrote:

"Death rather than dishonor" has been sublimely uttered by orators and novelists, but never was its import so heroically realized as in many instances like those daily occurring in prison. It was true that a few under terrible suffering, with death looking them in their faces, took the oath as the last hope of life. Yet I cannot but be amazed at the general constancy with which starving men repudiated such conduct while surrounded by suffering and death. There are but few instances recorded where men exposed to such temptations so resolutely acted, suffered, and died for the right.

The hero who gives his life for a cause, while shouts of comrades cheer his heart, thrilling with grand emotions, is looked upon with admiration. But he who suffers gradual starvation, temptation, and despair, for many, many weary

*Peter J. Edmonds was paroled at Wilmington, N.C., on Feb. 28th and reported to Camp Parole, Md., on March 29th. He was discharged for rheumatism and deafness at age 28 on May 9, 1865. No pension file exists.

months, and at last seals his devotion with death, is he not the truest hero?  Many a one lies to-day in his prison grave, which bears no name or mark to tell how he died, or what he suffered, or how true he was to the cause for which he renounced home, happiness, and life; but a grateful nation will recognize and remember in coming time the devotion which has done so much to perpetuate and preserve national life and honor."

Sgt. Eugene Forbes lies as an unknown in a mass grave at the site of  Florence Prison with 2,792 other Federal prisoners of war.

# Gallery of Portraits of Officers and Men
## of the
### 4th New Jersey Volunteer Infantry

**Second Lieutenant James Brewin**
(photo courtesy of Willaim B. Styple)

**Commissary Sergeant Leander Brewin**
(photo courtesy of William B. Styple)

**First Lieutenant William J. Cooke**
(photo courtesy of William B. Styple)

**Lieut. Colonel Charles Ewing**
(photo courtesy of USAMHI)

**Captain Samuel M. Gaul**
(photo courtesy of William B. Styple)

**Colonel William B. Hatch**
(photo courtesy of John Kuhl)

**Captain Horatio S. Howell**
(photo courtesy of William B. Styple)

**First Lieutenant Huntington W. Jackson**
(photo courtesy of William B. Styple)

**Captain Howard King**
(photo courtesy of John Kuhl)

**Captain Robert S. Johnston**
(photo courtesy of Marie Louise Stokes)

**Captain William McElhaney**
(photo courtesy of William B. Styple)

**Surgeon Joseph D. Osborne**
(photo courtesy of William B. Styple)

**Lieut. Colonel Brazilla Ridgway**
(photo courtesy of John Kuhl)

**Colonel James H. Simpson**
(photo courtesy of John Kuhl)

**First Lieutenant Josiah S. Studdiford**
(photo courtesy of NJ Archives)

# *Appendix* I

*Taken from the National Tribune*
**FUN AT MUNSON'S HILL**
**A Dummy Gun and Gunner**
**Appropriating Rebel Officers' Dinner**
**Capturing a Fort and Being Fired at.**
by Joseph Lawton
Co. B 4th NJV

Editor National Tribune: Where the rebels got their idea for the Quaker gun was at Camp Seminary, Va., where the 4th N.J. was in camp on the road leading to Mason's Hill. Co. B was stationed at a farm house between the picket line and the regiment. I, thinking to have a little fun, found a large piece of stovepipe in the barn, two wheels in the barnyard. The farm house had a flat roof. With a rope and a ladder I got the wheels and the stovepipe up on top of the house. I got an old pair of pants and an old blouse and stuffed them with straw. Then I got a piece of a shirt, and, with burnt wood, made the eyes, nose and mouth of a face, and fashioned a very respectable dummy, which I placed by the side of the wheels, with a stovepipe for the gun pointing toward the rebels. Munson's Hill being close by, our Captain, Wm. Seddon, saw that it was a good trick, so he got Ralph Owens to make a speech. The Captain first gave him a large drink of whiskey to get up steam, and then he went up the ladder and stood by the side of the wheels.   As he was speaking the company began to cheer, making a loud noise.  It so happened that Gen. McClellan was passing by at the time with his staff officers and about a regiment of cavalry.  As the General was passing he heard the noise and stopped, and with his field-glasses saw what was going on.  The guards at the gate told us that he and his staff officers laughed heartily at the dummy gun and gunner.

Our Captain had a large field-glass.  With it one could see the rebels standing on their breastworks in large numbers looking at the gun.   In a few days the company joined the regiment, and was sent out on picket duty close to Mason Hill. I, as Corporal, was stationed at the crossroads with six men. This was Sept. 28, 1861.  I got one man to go with me to see if we could find any rebels.  After going thru a woods we saw a farm house and I entered.   I asked the lady what the large table was for, and she said that the officers at the fort got their meals there, and that it was nearly time for them to come.  We went back, and told the Captain.  He got the company ready, and we went to the house and got the breakfast  intended for the rebels.   Then we went back to our picket line.  I got the idea that the rebels had gone, so with one man I got to the fort under cover of the fence and bushes.  We looked in and found no one in sight; then we hurried back.  I told the Captain about it, and he took half of the company, and we went inside the breastworks.  I found a mail bag full of letters from Richmond. Some of the letters I sent to Trenton and had printed in the papers.  We got a large rope that they had to tie their horses with, and after going thru the house we stood on the top of the breastworks and gave three cheers for Old Glory.  When we were going back thru a corn field we heard cheering at the breastworks. It was a regiment with a rebel flag. They opened fire, and the lead came after us like bees, but we got back safely to our picket line, which we held. I had blocked the road with evergreen trees early in the morning, and they were afraid to come near to it. About that time Gen. Kearny was out looking for hay for the horses, having the wagons and his brigade with him. He heard the firing, and came riding to the crossroads. He asked me what company I belonged to. I told him Co. B, 4th N.J. He asked me where my Captain was. I showed him Capt. Seddon in a field. The General got the regiments in line of battle, and our company advanced. As we were moving to the front, I was in the road. About that time an officer came riding up, his horse showing that he had been driving very fast, and asked me where Gen. Kearny was. Gen. Kearny was coming toward the fence at that moment, and as he jumped over landed near the officer that wanted to see him. Being nearby, I heard the officer say: "Gen. Kearny, Gen. McClellan doesn't want to bring on a battle so near the Capital, and his orders are to fall back a little, as the army is not ready." Gen. Kearny was mad when he heard this, and so was his regiment.

# *Appendix* II

*Taken from the National Tribune*
*Thursday, May 8, 1881*
**Crampton's Pass**
**And the Part Taken by the 4th New Jersey in that
Engagement.**
by John P. Beech
Co. B, 4th NJV

The rebels had a well directed artillery fire on our front and enfilading fire on our left flank from a battery posted on the mountain in front of where Smith's division was advancing. The rebels were posted behind a stone wall and about three hundred yards distant from our boys, in an open field. General Newton thought the distance was too great, so he ordered Torbert to charge forward with his second line, composed of the 3rd and 4th New Jersey. The order was given, and we bounded forward with a cheer. The other troops ceased firing, and we passed over them, and they immediately charged in our rear. The Johnnies broke and took shelter behind another stone wall near the base of the mountain, and here again we had it pretty warm for a while, when General Torbert ordered his brigade, composed of the 1st, 2d, 3d, and 4th New Jersey, to charge and drive them up the mountain. Col. Hatch, with the 4th, led the charge, followed immediately by the rest of the brigade.

In charging, the 4th New Jersey, which was on the left of the brigade, forced the rebel right back almost on their (the rebel) center, so that our line, as we drove them up the

mountain, was in the form of a semi-circle. Slowly, but
determinedly we pressed the enemy back, and as we neared
the crest of the mountain the fighting was desperate. The
rebels opened with grape and canister, killing and wounding
a good many of our boys, and among them our adjutant, a grape
shot passing through his body. But it was no time to falter, and
so, with a wild hurrah, we gained the crest, and the Johnnies
broke and fled down the western slope into Pleasant Valley.
As we had no cavalry we had to let them escape, as also a large
wagon train that was in sight. General Torbert was very
conspicuous in the fight. David Polk, company B, and Frank
Sanders, company F, each captured a stand of colors and we
ran  over another stand  which  was picked up by some
regiment in our rear.

For its conduct at this occasion the 4th New Jersey were
presented with a new State flag, containing a painting repre-
senting the regiment on a charge up the mountain and containing the following inscription:  "Presented by New Jersey to
her 4th regiment for gallant conduct at Crampton's Pass, Md.,
Sunday, September 14, 1862."  In our first charge Samuel
Hull, company B, was killed.  He was a good soldier and a
Christian; his prayer book was his constant companion and he
seemed to die murmuring a prayer as he fell.  Often, when he
would be detailed for fatigue on a Sunday, some of the boys
would volunteer in his place, knowing his reverence for the
day.  Just before our final charge on the mountain our orderly
sergeant- Jacob Ostermann- said to the boys, "Give it to them
boys; they killed our good old General Kearny."  The words
were hardly out of his mouth before he was wounded, but
before the sun went down he had the satisfaction of knowing
that we had given it to them in the very best style.  Our brigade

lost one commissioned officer killed and nine wounded, thirty-nine non-commissioned officers and privates killed and one hundred and twenty-five wounded--a total of one hundred and seventy-four.

On the 17th we marched to Antietam, and took position about 9 a.m. in front of the Dunker Church, in an open field, where there had been some fighting, and we fixed bayonets at one time to charge the woods, but the order was counter-manded. Later in the day our brigade was moved a few hundred yards further to the left on the left of the road heading to the church, to support some batteries. While here the following incident occurred: We were supporting two or three of our batteries when a rebel battery that was posted in the woods to the right (rebel) of the church opened, and it was surprising to see how the shot and shell was sent over and among us. The batteries that we were supporting had no show at all so they sent for Hexamer's battery A, 1st New Jersey. Soon he and his sturdy Germans appeared, and how the boys did cheer him as he double-quicked into position! "It silenced that battery or cut down every tree in the woods," was his reply to our boys. The other batteries ceased firing and Hexamer opened. For fifteen or twenty minutes, as fast as he could fire, he sent his shot and shell into and around that rebel battery, and the lines and trees crashed around them at such a rate that it sounded as if fifty ax-men were at work. Soon the rebel battery ceased to respond and then what a shout went up. Hexamer gave them ten or fifteen more as reminders for their insolence, and then withdrew his battery amid the cheers of all who witnessed the artillery duel.

A comrade told the writer that after the rebels fell back he saw the place which their battery had occupied, and that several of the pieces were dismounted, and broken trees and dead horses and dead artillerymen lay scattered around, showing the deadly effect of Hexamer's fire. After dark the writer with others was sent on the skirmish line, and after groping our way over and among dead and wounded comrades we got into position and I shall never forget the piteous appeals of the wounded on that occasion.

# *Appendix* III

## Company B at Spotsylvania.
### by John P. Beech

"About 5 A.M., we took up the line of march towards the right, but had not proceeded far before we about-faced and marched to the left, where we found that [Maj.Gen. Winfield Scott] Hancock with the 2nd Corps had charged upon and surprised the enemy, capturing the most of [Maj.-Gen. Edward] Johnson's Division with their artillery in their rifle pits with but small loss to Hancock. As we arrived on the field the Johnnies were rallying, and Hancock was falling back to the works. Our Brigade was halted and almost immediately the command came 'right-face', 'forward double-quick', 'march', and on the run we went about a quarter of a mile towards the right and came to halt in front of an angle in the works which were protected by an abatis of fallen trees. As we were double-quicking, a bullet sped through our ranks and Andrew Broughton of our company fell mortally wounded. In front of the works was an open field skirted on the left by an oak woods. We formed rapidly, and almost immediately the command was given to charge.

With a cheer we bounded forward, pushing and pulling away the abatis, and on to, and over the breastworks some of us went.    Pierson (of my company) and I mounted the breastworks together, and as we did so, I heard the fatal bullet, as Pierson clapped his hand to his side and started to the rear. Those of us who passed over the breastworks and into the clearing received a murderous fire from the oak woods, and from the enemy advancing through the clearing, and we had to beat a hasty retreat back to the works, but the Johnnies were right on top of us and captured several of our regiment, including John Duncan and William Jagers of my company. The latter had almost reached the woods when a piece of exploding shell struck his knapsack, whirling him around, and before he could recover himself, a Johnnie pulled him in. The Confederates now advanced until close to the works. Brigade after brigade was brought up around the spot and the fighting became desperate.  As I recrossed the breastworks, a section of the battery was being brought into position (Metcalf's section, Battery C, 5th U.S. Artillery) some of my regiment had to make way for them.  Horses and men began to go down before they were in position.  My regiment, pretty well mixed up in getting through the abatis had halted and were lying down, firing.  The fire was getting murderous and the enemy was preparing for a charge.  The battery was well up to the works, and was suffering severely.  Seeing the condition of affairs, I laid my musket down and appealed to Captain [Howard] King, Co. C (the only commissioned officer that I saw) to tell some of the men to get up and help work those guns, and I started to serve ammunition.  At this time there were but four rounds of canister left, after which we used shell. The battery was charged by a Mississippi Brigade who reached the works, but could get no further. Bullets were flying like hail stones, and with three men, we had to abandon the guns, which were later drawn out by a detail of our men. My regiment was ordered out by noon. Eight only of my company came out with the colors. We charged in with thirty-five men, five of whom were killed, fourteen wounded and two captured. Both commissioned officers were wounded. Our regimental loss was about one hundred, our Colonel being severely wounded, the command devolving on Captain Gaul. Our brigade sent further to the right, where the enemy were expecting to try to break through. There we remained all night, returning to the Angle the next day, when we buried our dead, at least those we could find. The field presented a sickening spectacle. Never before or after did I see such a slaughter in such a contracted place."

*John Beech received the medal of honor for his actions at Spotsylvania. In contrast, charges of cowardice were filled against Lt. Col. Charles Ewing after the battle stating: (Ewing) "did leave his regiment, when they were engaging the enemy and lie down and hide behind a tree and so remain until taken by the collar by Captain [John W.] Channing, 7th Maine Vols., and with kicks and cuffs driven up toward the position then occupied by his regiment."--Service record.*

# Appendix IV

### *Taken from,* The Andersonville Diary & Memoirs of Charles Hopkins, 1st New Jersey Infantry.

One day, while Stanton was employed on the wagon that made delivery of rations to camp-in the afternoon, after having been used in the forenoon, to cart the dead Yanks to the Cemetery.   Standing near the wagon was one of the ever-present "shadows." (So called, because starved to the limit of parchment and bones).  This man appealed most piteously to Stanton for a bone!  You may wonder why a bone, instead of meat, but there was more nourishment in the "cracked bone soup" than in the quantity of meat given and much healthier often, because of the quality of the meat.  Stanton's reply was "Yes, step up to the wagon and you will get a bunch of them." With Stanton standing in the wagon, the poor deluded fellow knew not his meaning, but confided in his word and stepped forward in a feeble effort to the rear of the wagon.  Towering over him was the cowardly Stanton.  The poor soul received a kick full in his mouth with the boot-shod foot, which not only cut his lips of the poor victim, but knocked out eight or ten teeth from the two jaws.  Hundreds saw, hooted, cursed and vented their full vocabulary of invective, but none dared touch him for the fear of results from the Confederates.  Of all the number who made protests, one had called him a coward, and other complimentary names.  To this one Stanton gave invitation to step forward and he could have some of the same treatment. I refused to accept. Stanton jumped to the ground and said, "You will fight me for this and God Damn you, I will kill you, fight or not!!!" The battle was for my life, I knew, cool of head with catlike swiftness of movement, skillful as to my hands, I soon placed the strong brute in darkness with a bloody face.

# Bibliography

UNPUBLISHED MATERIAL

Dennis Buttacavoli Collection
  Robert Aitken letters.
John Kuhl Collection
  John Beech diary.
Joseph Bilby Collection
  Samuel Hull/ Eugene Forbes letters.
Marie Louise Stokes Collection
  Capt. Robert S. Johnston letters.

National Archives, Washington D.C.
  Military Service & Pension Records
  Regimental Records

PUBLISHED SOURCES
NEWSPAPERS

Trenton Public Library, Trenton, N.J.
  Special Collections
    Daily State Gazzette
Library of Congress, Washington D.C.
  National Tribune

BOOKS

Atwater, Dorence. *List of Prisoners Who Died in 1864-65 at Andersonville Prison.* Andersonville, Ga.: National Society of Andersonville, 1981.

Baquet, Camille, *History of the First Brigade, New Jersey Volunteers.* Trenton: MacCrellish & Quigley, 1910.

Beyer, W.F. *Deeds of Valor from Records in the Archives of the United States Government.* Detroit, 1907.

Foster, John Y. *New Jersey and the Rebellion.* Newark: Dennis & Co., 1868.

Goss, Warren Lee. *The Soldier's Story of His Captivity at Andersonville, Belle Isle, and Other Rebel Prisons.* Boston: L.N. Richardson, 1873.

Hunt, Roger D., Jack R. Brown. *Brevet Brigadier Generals in Blue.* Gaithersburg, MD: Olde Soldier Books, 1990.

Long, E.B. *The Civil War Day By Day.* New York: Doubleday, 1971.

Morton, Joseph W., editor. [Charles F. Currie accounts] *Sparks from the Campfire.* Philadelphia: Keystone Publishing Co., 1892.

Hopkins, C.F., R.A. Clark. *Report of the New Jersey Andersonville Monument Commissioners.* Somerville, NJ: Unionist-Gazzette Assoc., 1899.

Stryker, William S. *Record of Officers and Men of New Jersey in the Civil War 1861-1865.* Trenton: Murphy Steam Book and Job Printer, 1876.

Styple, William B., John Fitzpatrick, eds. *The Andersonville Diary and Memoirs of Charles Hopkins, 1st New Jersey Infantry.* Kearny, N.J.: Belle Grove Publishing Co., 1988.

Toombs, Samuel. *New Jersey Troops in the Gettysburg Campaign.* Orange, NJ: Evening Mail Publishing House, 1888.

Warner, Ezra J. *Generals in Blue.* Baton Rouge: Louisiana State University Press, 1964.

# Picture Credits

Page 20: Meridith Havens Fire & Civil War Museum, Trenton, N.J.  29: Marie Louise Stokes.  30: Trenton Public Library, Trenton, N.J.  45: USAMHI/MASS. MOLLUS, Carlisle, PA.  51: USAMHI; John Kuhl.  53: National Tribune.  60: USAMHI.  93: American Heritage.  97: USAMHI.  98: American Heritage.  106: USAMHI.  108: USAMHI.  114: American Heritage.

# Index